PHIL TAYLOR-GUCK

THE AI ALARM BELL

ARTIFICIAL INTELLIGENCE AND HOW TO SAVE HUMAN CULTURE BEFORE IT'S TOO LATE

R^ethink

First published in Great Britain in 2026
by Rethink Press (www.rethinkpress.com)

Contents

Introduction

There's a game I used to play with my children when they were a lot younger as I walked with them to junior school. It's called the 'why' game. If you've never tried it before, it goes like this: I'd start the conversation with something like, 'What have you got on today?'

ANSWER: Maths.

ME: Why?

ANSWER: Because I have to do it.

ME: Why?

ANSWER: The teacher says so.

ME: Why?

ANSWER: To pass my exams.

ME: Why?

ANSWER: To get a good job.

You get the picture. Often, during the fifteen-minute walk, the successive *whys* took us to space and the outer regions of the universe. What I really like about it is that young children are just so inciteful with their answers. This is not just a proud father speaking. All preschool and early primary-age kids are very sharp, indeed. Developmental psychologists call it the 'why' stage, and kids' questions are their primary tool for learning and sense-making. The questions might sound unfiltered, but they are unerringly pertinent and we should listen to them a bit more often. Innately, they absolutely get why it's important to keep asking why. Very quickly, however, the system makes them put their hands up to ask questions. This naturally slows down the *whys* and, over time, kids learn to fit in and follow the path they are told to follow. The impulse towards divergent thinking drops off a cliff: in one longitudinal study, 98% of participating 5-year-olds achieved genius-level scores on a creativity test for thinking like this, but by age 10, the genius-level scores dropped to 30%.[1] Sadly, unless they're encouraged by an outside source to continue to question *everything*, young people often become less inquisitive and, therefore, less creative.

Asking *why* about AI

I've made a big effort to keep the 'why' game going with my now-teenage children. Over time, I've listened as their perspective of the world has gradually changed. We still never shy away from the big subjects. The big subject I am most interested in at the moment is AI and its potential impact on society, which is why I have been quietly playing the 'why' game myself. Society is going through enormous changes right now, primarily because of advances in technology, mostly AI-led. Today, the younger generations' answers to any *why* question about what comes next seem as good as, or even better than, the responses many of the so-called experts are coming up with, if these adults question where it all ends at all.

My conclusion is that not enough people are thinking 'what next?' or questioning how we, as humans, should be shaping our future in an increasingly digital world, despite all indications suggesting that the time to do so is right now. Arguably, we should have started asking *why* about AI years ago.

We are, without a doubt, in the midst of one of the biggest transformations of our economic and social outlook in human history, if not *the* biggest. While many are quick to celebrate the positives of technology, few seem willing to admit that what is currently happening points to an uncertain, unstable future. As kids, we were brought up to believe our lives would be better than our parents', just as their lives turned out better than their own parents'. Now, for the first time in generations, this is not necessarily the case. What will parents tell their kids when they ask why this has happened? How will the current generations of adults equip the next ones for what lies ahead?

What we are seeing now has to be properly questioned because it is something completely new. Technology will govern every aspect of our lives. As an entrepreneur, I am most interested in the working environment and how this will change. As a starting point, I found it helpful to delve back into the history books to properly understand the current pace of change and why we need to be prepared for the profound impact it will have on all of our lives.

The five sectors of work

For centuries, human civilisation has been organised around sectors of work. Things have changed along the way. That's progress, after all. Yet each new stage has mostly made a positive impact on how people lived, what they valued and how entire societies were structured. Economists in the 20th century divided the most profound periods of change in working practices into three sectors: primary, secondary and tertiary. Two further sectors, quaternary and quinary, were added later. Together, these five sectors are quite a useful way to understand the progression.

The beginning of the primary sector is the foundation of life itself. Think here of agriculture, hunting, fishing, forestry and mining: pursuits that dominated human activity for millennia. Work was physical, bound to the rhythms of Earth and the seasons. Any gains in productivity, like the inventions of the plough or irrigation systems, were big steps forward that allowed populations to grow. Nevertheless, a balance between human brainpower and (mostly) muscle remained the core driver of economic life.

Fast forward to the Industrial Revolution, which began in the mid-18th century, and all of that changed. Steam, coal, steel – and, later, electricity and assembly lines – are the foundations on which the secondary sector was built. Advances in engineering and science spurred mass production on a scale never seen before. Workers were drawn away from the countryside and into smoke-belching factories that proliferated in rapidly growing cities. After hundreds of years of status quo, this progress heralded a social and economic shift. The only thing that didn't change much was the small number of people who benefited massively from the unparalleled wealth that the surge in production created. For those workers who had swapped the autonomy of the farm for the discipline of the factory floor, life became a little better, but it was still clock-driven and, now, machine-regimented. The shift remade class structures and family life, but it wasn't great for the masses, or indeed, the environment.

The next big shift in the working world came far quicker than the previous one. By the mid-20th century, services took a dominant economic role and the tertiary sector began. In this sector, labour demand in the service sector, which previously required tens of thousands of factory workers, expanded to millions of positions in a variety of services. This included workers in shops, healthcare, banking, education, entertainment and administration. The most-prized skills in the jobs market were related to engaging with others, including smooth interactions, persuasive ability and empathy. During this time, doctors, teachers and lawyers became the most highly respected professionals, and all were paid accordingly.

Everything changed again when the quaternary sector began, even sooner, with the emergence of the knowledge economy. By the 1970s, just a few decades after the start of the service-sector boom, the most valuable resource had become information. For those seeking the biggest pay cheques, the jobs to aim for were in research, data analysis, software development and consulting. Just as quickly, careers in medicine or education became devalued, reflected by falling wages in real terms. (Lawyers have managed to hang on to their position in the upper echelons – for the time being at least.) The quaternary sector was the age of the office park and the digital revolution, where work became less about physical presence and more about what you knew and how quickly you could apply it. Intellectual capital replaced physical capital as the defining force of growth.

The quinary sector is where we find ourselves now. Today, the working world is focused on the highest levels of decision-making and creativity. Tech entrepreneurship and innovation have emerged as the most highly prized career paths, and to be among the tiny handful who make it big, you need exceptional judgement, vision and imagination. We all know their names: Musk, Bezos, Zuckerberg, Gates and Altman. Some of us might know a small tier of names below them. The sky is the limit on how much this small group can earn, with fortunes running into the billions while salaries stagnate in real terms elsewhere. Those who make it to the highest level use their insights to steer corporations, governments and, indeed, much of what the rest of us do day-to-day.

Transformations of the quinary sector

We're already seeing ample evidence of the transformations tech bros are directing from Silicon Valley. It's everywhere you look. Take resource allocation as an example. The technologies Silicon Valley has built can allocate resources with no human interaction required. Global finance is shaped by automated systems with barely any input from human traders. Indeed, high-frequency trading platforms account for the majority of equity trades in markets like those in the UK and US, executing thousands of transactions in microseconds – too fast for any person to monitor, let alone control. In logistics, Amazon's supply chain is coordinated by algorithms that dynamically reroute inventory, anticipate demand and allocate stock with a precision that no team of managers could achieve, no matter their efficiency with a spreadsheet.

Elsewhere, we're also seeing knowledge creation by machines. Large language models generate research papers, draft legal contracts and make extraordinary medical advances. In 2020, DeepMind's AlphaFold solved the 'protein-folding problem' that brilliant scientists had battled with for fifty years. For those who are curious, the issue that had stumped scientists was predicting how a protein's long chain of amino acids will fold into a precise three-dimensional shape that determined how the protein functions. Tiny changes in folding can radically alter behaviour, so understanding this unlocked insights into the biological machinery of life. This paved the way for a breakthrough that will accelerate drug discovery and reshape biotech. The breakthrough allows researchers to identify the mechanisms that drive some diseases and paves the way for far more effective designer medicines. Already, pharmaceutical companies are partnering with AI firms to generate compounds for clinical trials. This sort of work used to take human specialists years of painstaking research.

It is almost impossible to count the ways automated decision-making is creeping into everyday life. Algorithms decide who gets everything from bank loans to parole. Applicant-tracking systems filter job candidates so efficiently that, chances are, when you fill out an application the first eyes on it won't be eyes at all, but a model that scores you before a human ever sees your name. In medicine, AI is being trialled to prioritise which patients receive scarce resources such as transplant organs. Even the less-than-cutting-edge world of politics is getting in on the act. Governments are experimenting with predictive analytics to shape public policy from crime prevention to welfare distribution. Each of these systems is doing much more than advising human decision-makers. Increasingly, they make the first, and sometimes the final, cut.

The post-quinary sectors

The possibilities of where we will go in the post-quinary sectors are seemingly endless. Until now, economies have been designed around our human needs, ambitions and constraints, taking into account our 'weaknesses', or inability to work 24/7. AI does not need sleep or weekends off or an annual holiday to recharge itself. This also means it can scale at levels otherwise unimaginable for individuals, and even organisations.

Just consider the work-sector changes that are predicted to come next. (As you are looking through the following predictions, bear in mind that the pace of change will almost certainly accelerate with each, as it always has to date.) In the emerging post-quinary sectors, we will see a rapid and complete transfer of agency from humans to machines.

At the moment, a bit of guesswork is involved in how this will unfold. Futurists and business thinkers have named the sectors that will follow the quinary based on their forecasts for each stage and the number sequence of the previous five. Though no one knows the exact sequence of events, it looks like a logical flow to me.

The senary sector, is expected to centre around autonomous production. Goods will no longer be created by people working in factories, or even by human-supervised robots, but by entirely self-directing systems. Supply chains won't wait for managers to make adjustments; they'll shoulder the task of optimising them-selves in real time. No human agency will be required.

By the septenary sector, we'll have reached the synthetic intelligence economy, and algo-rithms will direct all new knowledge. Input from human scientists, designers or writers will no longer be required. Machines will produce research, design and even cultural artefacts without any input from us.

In the octonary sector, we will be living in a machine-to-machine economy. Machines will trade, negotiate and transact with one another, optimising themselves to meet goals that may have been set by real people at one time, but that was the extent of the human role. Machines will operate in ways we cannot directly oversee because they developed the operations and know them best.

By the nonary sector, these theorists anticipate that we will have relinquished our say in how we live our lives altogether. In this sector, a new system of autonomous governance will tear apart the historical and deeply held assumption that humans alone should decide how our societies should be ordered. Algorithms will take charge of distributing resources, enforcing compliance and even determining what is 'fair', based on what they decide are more efficient. Of course, their autonomy will also mean they are less accountable for the decisions they make.

The final sector, the denary, is perhaps the most alarming of all. Here, AI is sentient and poses the most profound break to date with everything that went before. In this world, machines are not simply tools but actors in their own right, with their own forms of agency and perhaps preferences or rights. In the denary sector, people will no longer be the sole participants in the economy, but one among many intelligent entities.

Industrialised intelligence: Planning ahead

The scale and speed by which all this may happen is almost as hard to comprehend as the scope. What we are about to experience is so much more than a few chapters in the history of economic change or the logical, step-by-step progress we've all grown used to in our lifetimes. We are racing towards the first time in history that the central actor in economic life is no longer human. Algorithms, automated platforms and intelligent systems are already smoothly slipping into roles we once saw as uniquely ours.

Right now, we have no idea what will be unleashed when intelligence itself becomes industrialised. It is almost too big to imagine what might happen to labour or society itself when we are no longer at the centre of it all. All we know is that we are stepping into an entirely radical era where all territory is uncharted. The question is no longer just how well and quickly humans will adapt to new tools, but what happens when the tools themselves set the terms of adaptation. If the primary to quinary sectors represent the story of how human ingenuity shaped the world we know today, the unfolding post-quinary sectors may well represent the story of how human ingenuity is challenged, and perhaps even overshadowed, by its own creations.

Labour implications

The implications of industrialised intelligence on labour are enormous. If knowledge work can be automated, then even professions once considered 'future-proof' may no longer be secure. Until now, one of the few things individuals and, indeed, entire economies have been able to truly bank on is the value of capability. Skills have always been more than simply tools of production. They were a sure-fire route to opportunity and the most dependable hedge against the unknown. What will become of lawyers, consultants or executives when algorithms can outperform them in speed, accuracy and cost? How will societies organise themselves when the central promise of the knowledge and quinary economies – that a degree-level education and white-collar expertise guarantee stable employment – no longer holds true?

There will be implications all the way down the line in the job market, with both skilled and unskilled labour. Young people will be left with a narrowing horizon, which will mostly involve precarious gig jobs, zero-hour contracts and low pay. The reduction in prospects will inevitably erode the social fabric that binds communities together. We're just at the beginning of this change, and the consequences are already abundantly visible across the UK, particularly in towns and regions that were once powered by skilled hands-on work. Today, many of those once-prosperous places have become known for joblessness or underemployment, sadly often leading to civic disengagement when the people who live in these areas feel like they have no options. Inevitably, this disengagement grows from generation to generation.

Shaping our own future

AI is not simply another sectoral shift, like moving from farms to factories or from factories to offices. Each of the transformations shaping the first five sectors, as disruptive as they were, relied on human beings at their core. AI represents something different. It is capable of assuming tasks once thought to be inseparable from human intelligence. The true impact is only just beginning to show, but we are already seeing the world beginning to operate in ways that position humans not as indispensable participants, but optional supervisors. Increasingly, we are becoming bystanders.

Many of AI's advances will be positive, of course, and we've already seen evidence of this, too. However, many advances won't be positive, and those are the ones I'm concerned with in this book. We can't assume that someone, somewhere, will act in our best interests to ensure everything works out alright in the end. There is certainly no point waiting for the tech giants to put up guardrails ensuring that any of the developments they are pushing through are to all our advantages – or at least not to our detriment. It is not in their interests to do so. They are motivated by power and money. There are few companies that would give that up for the good of society.

My view, therefore, is that we need to play an active role in shaping our future before it is shaped for us. To do this, we need to ask an awful lot of *why* questions, interrogating where we are going and whether it is the right direction. We need to better understand accountability, fairness and trust, which means asking why we are blindly walking into a world where the most powerful actor in the economy is not human. Why is no one talking about the risks involved with slipping into the role of spectator and watching as the future evolves with little regard for us?

My reason for writing this book is to begin to explore some of these questions. As the title suggests, the alarm bells are ringing, and we urgently need to think about our response. This is not about seeing off the 'threat' of technology. I love technology. I've been fascinated by AI since before any of the commercial systems launched. Since they became available, I have used ChatGPT for anything and everything. While I know and understand its capabilities, I also believe that there's a false sense of security among the many users who seem to assume AI will solve all workforce issues or that it is the answer to every challenge. The reality is much more nuanced. We need to work those nuances out, though, or we will easily lose control.

Let's play the 'why' game.

The Illusion Of Permanence

Every major technological and economic rupture, bar none, has been preceded by a period of blissful overconfidence that things will always be this way. It's not wilful ignorance; we have been hard-wired to find comfort in continuity since our ancient ancestors lived in caves and relied on the patterns in seasons, food sources and social hierarchies to survive. Today, the belief that our way of life will largely stay the same acts as a psychological anchor in an unpredictable world. This feeling of stability allows us to make plans and imagine the future as an extension of the present. If we couldn't rely on this solid foundation, everyday life would feel just a bit too fragile.

Our attachment to permanence is often reinforced by long stretches of relative stability, explaining why disruptions – whether sudden industry collapse, financial crises or technological revolutions – feel like existential ruptures, not just economic shocks. They threaten the very idea that the future is secure and predictable.

Seismic shifts, seismic fallout

Let's return briefly to the secondary sector. Imagine what it was like to live through the upheaval of the Industrial Revolution. Until that time, generation after generation had assumed that agriculture would always remain the backbone of the economy. Farming had been the dominant human activity seemingly forever, employing the vast majority of the population and underpinning the structure of entire societies. It is almost certain that when early industrial machinery began to appear, from steam engines to mechanical looms, many people were quick to dismiss it as a curiosity that could never replace human hands in the fields or craft workshops. It would have been difficult to imagine a world where less than even half the population farmed, let alone less than 5%, as is the case in advanced economies today.

As we now know, the implications of overturning these assumptions were seismic. Within a century of the Industrial Revolution, millions had left rural areas for crowded factory towns and cities, where the housing, sanitation and public health infrastructure was woefully unprepared. Traditional skills lost their value almost overnight, and whole classes of skilled artisans, once thought indispensable, were displaced, leaving entire communities to fall into poverty. The disruption was not temporary; agriculture's importance to the economy had been permanently diminished, and it took generations for society to adjust.

This scenario repeated with the same resulting seismic shocks at the dawn of the quaternary sector. For much of the early 20th century, industrial jobs in coal, steel, ship-building and car-making were bedrocks of prosperity. The jobs on offer involved tough, often dirty, work, but they also guaranteed a steady wage, and workers in these industries believed that they had 'jobs for life'. In some cases, entire regional identities grew around the certainty that steel mills, coal mines or car plants would always be there. Once again, however, these beliefs and identities unravelled at a breathtaking pace, this time in the 1970s and 80s, when globalisation, cheap overseas labour and automation hollowed out these industries. Plants closed and mines shut down, and the communities that relied on them plunged into unemployment and despair. As with the Industrial Revolution, it took decades for economies and societies to adapt, a process that continues today, as some regions have reinvented themselves around services, finance or technology, while others remain trapped in decline.

The belief that these industries would always provide jobs, coupled with the failure to predict and manage change, proved disastrous, and we are still dealing with the political consequences even now. Countless communities feel deep resentment towards the so-called elites who appear to have benefited the most from pursuing the next shiny thing without so much as a backward glance at the industries they abandoned in their wake. The distrust of globalisation and rising populist movements we're seeing today can be traced, at least in part, to the failure to manage the economic rupture of the quaternary sector.

Warning bells unheeded

These lessons should be a warning bell as AI's rise gathers pace. Just as centres of heavy industry shuttered almost overnight once new supply chains and technologies made them obsolete, entire categories of white-collar work could disappear as algorithms begin to handle research, analysis, design and even judgement. Even though this has already begun, we continue to operate on the assumption that careers in law, consultancy and medicine will continue to be central to economic life. These are our 21st-century equivalent of 'jobs for life': jobs believed to be too skilled, and too bound up with identity and stability, to ever vanish. As I've shown, this assumption is ill-advised, but there is little sign of any significant attempt to stave off the coming upheaval. Quite the opposite, in fact. We still blindly follow the same script when guiding young people's aspirations: work hard at school and you'll be able to go to college, achieve all your aspirations and walk into a high paying white-collar career.

Over the past fifty or so years, the numbers of students in higher education have soared. In 1970, just 8% of young people chose this route, but by 1990, that number had more than doubled to 19%.[2] Today, that number is around 36%, slightly down from 38% in 2021.[3] The surge in university attendance has been driven, in large part, by government policy. After Tony Blair swept into power in 1997, one of his priorities was to improve standards of education. He later said it was crucial to help create a 21st-century nation based not on privilege, class or background, but the equal worth of all.[4] He set an ambitious target of 50% for young adults entering higher education in this century.

With university not just encouraged but the default option, degree inflation took hold. So many young people come onto the job market with degrees, that employers say it is too difficult to distinguish between them. Now young people are being encouraged to stay on at university even longer to obtain a master's qualification so that, in a graduate-saturated labour market, they stand out among their counterparts with only a common or garden-variety degree. This market saturation is exacerbated by the fact that so many young adults choose degrees in largely similar subjects. Universities turn out waves of graduates in law, psychology and media. As a result, even with master's-level qualifications, many graduates are finding themselves underemployed or working in fields completely unrelated to their original studies. Meanwhile, AI is steadily eroding jobs in highly educated fields such as law, psychology and media.

At the same time, governments throughout the political divide appear never to have questioned why we continue to relentlessly drive young people from school to university in order to apply for jobs that simply may not be there when they graduate. It is glaringly apparent that young people today are being sold a story that no longer holds any worth. They are being encouraged to pursue degree paths for the supposed doors they will open to white-collar 'jobs for life', but for many, the doors lead only to temporary contracts, stagnant wages, and a return to the family home post-graduation. Of course, there also is the financial aspect to the whole charade. Average graduate debt now exceeds £53,000,[5] and as the number of available jobs dwindle, the graduate wage premium narrows year-on-year.[6]

So why do we keep pushing people towards jobs that will almost certainly not exist in the next decade, possibly sooner? I suspect we do so because we are determined to continue believing in the service and knowledge economies as permanent safe havens for human work, reinforced by the cultural narratives we build and willingly subscribe to. Films, literature and journalism often depicted robots as machines of physical labour, not thinkers and, when they do think, their thought processes are directed by us. We have been operating under a comfortable assumption of irreducible human superiority. It may be possible to replace a weaver or a miner with a machine, this line of thinking goes, but never a surgeon or a strategist.

This unwavering faith that it will all work out just fine, with life continuing as normal, over-looks two critical realities. The first is that much of what we call 'knowledge work' relies on pattern recognition, rule-following and infor-mation processing, all skills at which machines are already entirely proficient. The second, per-haps less obvious, reality is that the boundary between human and machine capability has never been set in stone; it shifts whenever tech-nology improves. One by one, as technology improves, the safe havens of uniquely human behaviours turn out not so safe after all.

Will the future have lawyers?

Law has long been held as the quintessential safe profession. It has already survived many economic and labour shifts from one sector to the next. What has kept this profession out of the crosshairs of major social changes is that legal practice has always been about more than simple rules on a page. The law of the day requires interpretation, argument, persuasion and an intimate grasp of human complexity. Lawyers are skilled in reading between the lines, detecting nuance and weighing competing claims of justice. Surely, the thinking went, no machine could replicate the craft of cross-examination or the delicate art of negotiation. For decades, this assumption went unchallenged. Law firms – and, indeed, legal fees – multiplied, and the industry became a pillar of middle-class and elite employment. Young people who performed well at school were ushered towards a 'future-proof' career in law. The more complex the world becomes, they thought, the more work lawyers would have.

You don't need to look too carefully to see that the cracks in this thinking are already showing in the AI era. First, there were the software tools that could search legal databases far faster than any junior associate, reducing the need for armies of them to sift through case law. E-discovery platforms soon followed, capable of scanning millions of documents for relevant evidence at speeds no human could match. Once machine learning entered the field, efficiency software expanded into contract-drafting systems that can predict the outcomes of legal action and generate legal briefs. Now start-ups like DoNotPay[7] position themselves as 'robot lawyers', automating claims for parking tickets, airline compensation and small disputes – tasks once reserved for junior- or entry-level practitioners. In more complex domains, AI models now assist judges and barristers by highlighting precedents, flagging contract risks and modelling cases' likely cost and duration.

This is all happening now. The legal profession's very foundation and promise as a human-only sanctuary have been shaken. There are still roles for senior partners as a physical presence in the courtroom or to give strategic oversight to clients, but they are greatly diminished. Meanwhile, for the large number of graduates who have been ushered towards law, the path into the profession has narrowed substantially. The traditional apprenticeship, in which junior associates learn by doing the painstaking grunt work of research and drafting, is being eaten away by automation. Further, the assumptions that judgement, interpretation and reasoning are uniquely human domains are being tested daily.

Broader implications

Medicine, like law, has long been assumed beyond the reach of automation because it relies on qualities perceived as uniquely human, such as empathy. There's also a belief that the subtle art of diagnosis is grounded in lived experience. In many ways, medicine has been seen, historically, as an even safer career than law. It is a universally respected, highly paid profession that until recently was shielded from excessive mechanisation. Yet medicine is now also being reconfigured by data-driven systems. For example, the field of radiology, once considered a pinnacle of specialist expertise, has been a proving ground for AI, with algorithms now matching or surpassing human experts in identifying tumours, fractures and certain diseases. Diagnostic tools powered by machine learning can now analyse thousands of patient records, spotting patterns any individual physician would be hard-pressed to find. With each passing year, AI is increasingly trusted to take on tasks that were previously the domain of qualified doctors and nurses. AI-assisted triage systems now determine who is seen first in hospitals, and predictive models shape decisions about which treatments to pursue. These developments don't eliminate doctors, but they do radically alter their role, shifting doctors' focus from routine analysis to oversight of machine outputs. Thus, the once-safe domain of medicine loses its immunity to the relentless march of AI and is reshaped at its core.

There's a similar story around finance. The superpowers needed to succeed in this highly competitive and well-paid industry are judgement, intuition and experience, all human skills that could not possibly be replicated by machines – could they? Traders, for example, have traditionally prided themselves on their sharp instincts, and fund managers work hard to cultivate reputations as market sages. But these roles are already changing. Financial markets are increasingly dominated by algorithmic and high-frequency trading platforms, executing millions of trades in microseconds, far faster than any human. Risk models assess portfolios with precision unattainable through intuition. Credit decisions, once made by a banker who knew the client, are now made by credit-scoring systems that weigh hundreds of variables and make decisions instantly. Even venture capital, a field supposedly built on gut instinct and networking, is increasingly influenced by data-driven scouting tools that root out promising start-ups long before human investors notice them. The mythology around the city as the domain of human brilliance is giving way to a new reality in which machines do much of the decisive work.

The developments in law, medicine and finance have a lot in common, including disrupting the misplaced assumption that job complexity equates to job security. For decades, people believed that if you had a job requiring judgement, whether it be judgement over what happened with our lives or money, that profession was untouchable. We now know that judgement qualities are exactly what AI excels at. In fact, machines are better than us when it comes to spotting patterns in data, reasoning through problems and analysing rule-based structures. Career options that perform these types of tasks are no longer safe from technological advance. In fact, they are built on a house of cards.

Creativity: AI's next front

Ah, you may be thinking, *there is one area where the machines can't excel: creativity.* This ability is what makes us unique. Machines can calculate, recall and execute, but they could never be designed to imagine, empathise or create new and original ideas. For the most part, the arts have never been seen as a strong entry point to white-collar jobs, though media, design and marketing have always had a big draw. But can we assume that careers founded in creativity, which rely on human intuition and original-ity, are the safe haven many are seeking? The answer, I am afraid to say, is no.

Once again, our assumptions are being eroded. Generative AI systems are already producing novels, screenplays, advertising copy, music and visual art at scales and speeds that were once unthinkable. They can use previously produced work to mimic existing styles and blend influences in the blink of an eye, testing hundreds of iterations and adapting to feedback in real time. Advertising agencies are using AI to generate entire campaign concepts and optimise ad timing and placement. In film and television, script-writing AI tools are achieving co-writer status. Special effects, whose creation once required a huge workforce, have begun to be automated. Even journalism, a career once emblematic of the creative knowledge economy, is increasingly shaped by AI, which has taken over a wide range of tasks, including drafting financial reports and sports updates and trawl-ing vast datasets for investigative leads.

The economics of this shift are decisive. Why pay a human designer for weeks of work when an AI can create hundreds of viable concepts in an afternoon? Industries once thought safe are beginning to see their workflows reorganised around AI tools, and we've already seen mass redundancies, since fewer people are needed to achieve the same output. For example, in September 2025, Reach, the publisher of national titles like *The Mirror, Express* and *Star*, as well as scores of regional titles, announced hundreds of redundancies in a restructure aimed at adapting to 'changing reader habits and the impact of artificial intelligence.'[8] There is also evidence of mass layoffs at TV and film studios. While the entertainment groups behind the layoffs have not explicitly framed them as AI-related, it is telling that the 2023 wave of Writers Guild and SAG-AFTRA strikes in Hollywood were in large part about protecting creators from indiscriminate AI use.[9] Meanwhile, in advertising, it is forecast that 7.5% of agency jobs will be replaced by AI by 2030.[10]

Humanity's last bastion … for now

Some elements of creativity remain stubbornly resistant to automation, at least for now. The ability to surprise in ways that feel genuinely new, not just statistically novel, is still uniquely human. Deeply human qualities such as lived experience, cultural nuance and emotional resonance are also hard for machines to replicate.

Think of a novel rooted in a childhood memory of migration or a painting inspired by grief or a comedy routine that captures the subtleties of a particular common situation. Each of these draw from reservoirs of meaning that no dataset can entirely encode. Creativity, like beauty, is in the eye of the beholder, making it difficult for AI to replicate on a broad scale. In addition, audiences often crave not just the creative work, but the story behind it, seeking deeper connection with the person who made it. That narrative context gives human-made work a depth that algorithms, however sophisticated, cannot yet supply.

For the moment, the debate centres around whether AI can ever be truly creative. If it generates a compelling image or writes a moving piece of text but uses sources created by humans, is it creative? Is creativity simply the act of producing something novel that resonates, regardless of who or what produces it? As the boundaries between the contributions of human and machine blur, these questions become less relevant and more a distraction from what is happening. We know for certain that assuming creative industries are immune to automation is another version of a familiar mistake. Just as lawyers, doctors and financiers once imagined their expertise would remain indispensable, artists, writers and creators may find that in their fields, too, human ingenuity ultimately competes with, adapts to, or is amplified by machine imagination.

Human creativity may not experience blanket replacement, but it will undergo a restructuring that will see the options for creative careers vastly diminished. Machines will continue to colonise the repetitive, scalable and time-sensitive parts of creative work, while humans will funnel into a diminishing number of roles that emphasise originality, curation and the intangible spark of lived experience. The safe havens will simply prove temporary refuges until technology catches up.

TWO

Searching For Winners

The World Economic Forum's 2023 Future of Jobs report makes for gloomy reading. It projects that by 2027, 85 million jobs globally will be displaced by AI and automation, while only 69 million new roles are expected to emerge in return.[11] Many of those new roles will not be linear upgrades from the old ones, but will demand a complex blend of technical literacy, cross-functional teamwork, digital fluency and hands-on operational skills that our current workforce, trained primarily for a specific single profession, are simply not equipped to deliver. Given these factors, it's a wise time investment to start thinking about which sectors will offer those 69 million new roles. Certainly, any young person entering university would be ill-advised to aim for professions that will contribute to the 85 million jobs we expect to shed.

The wave of automation will hit from the top down. In the past, low-wage, low-skill workers bore the brunt of technological shifts such as the rise of industrial automation or mechanised agriculture. This time, it will be desk workers and mid-level professionals facing obsolescence, with white-collar workers the most vulnerable. Knowledge work, once seen as the safest bet for upward mobility, is already under attack from automation and artificial intelligence, and the more routine and replicable the work, the more susceptible it is to AI substitution. For workers who are already on the career ladder and have invested heavily in degrees, this is terrible news, threatening both income and identity.

However, there is still time for those who have not yet entered the workplace to adjust their path toward roles that won't be quickly supplanted by AI. To fully understand the terrain, we need to explore which jobs are most likely to endure, specifically, which tasks or roles AI fundamentally struggles to replicate. These roles resist codification because they rely on uniquely human aptitudes. What AI can do is transformative: it can generate text, power chatbots, scan large datasets and run factory production lines. What it can't do – at least not economically or at scale – is credibly replicate skilled roles or human qualities such as care and empathy.

Skilled roles, human strengths

Let's start with skilled roles that require the expertise of tradespeople, such as electricians, plumbers or carpenters. Professions like these depend on a unique blend of physical problem-solving and in-the-moment judgement, often under unpredictable and imperfect conditions. This is especially so in the UK, where much of the built environment – whether rail, utilities, housing or public buildings – dates back decades if not centuries. These sites are layered with legacy materials, irregular layouts and unpredictable variables. Attempting to deploy autonomous robotics on infrastructure that was never designed to accommodate them is fraught with complications. Maybe that will change one day, but that day is definitely not now.

AI has its place, of course. However, it lacks *embodied intelligence*, or the physical and spatial intuition human workers develop through years of practice. Robots and AI also struggle with ambiguity, messiness and novelty. Think of the types of building or repair work that buildings in the UK need, even those dating back a decade or so. The skilled tradespeople who work in our housing and commercial property sectors often need to navigate uneven flooring, cramped roof spaces and years-old building quirks. These buildings are a very long way from the types of clean labs or tidy digital environments that are essential for robots to work efficiently. Our skilled workers need to be able to solve problems that manuals don't cover, because every site, job and repair has its own hidden variables. A dripping pipe might seem simple until the experienced plumber working on it notices that it runs through walls from a previous renovation or that the stopcock hasn't moved since 1964.

To work onsite in unpredictable situations, dexterity, sensory awareness and contextual understanding are critical. Consider what is required for a worker to detect the faint hiss of a gas leak or identify faulty wiring by smell or heat. Consider the complexities of installing a boiler in a 1930s council flat where space is tight, materials are worn and access is limited. How would you go about troubleshooting a complex fault on a solar inverter system while working on a slippery roof in gusty weather? These are not the types of conditions under which robots thrive, even without considering the countless other variables they would have to contend with. Trade work is full of improvisation, for example, cutting a bespoke joint by hand when factory parts don't fit, adapting on the fly to new site conditions or working around the unpredictable legacies of previous substandard repairs.

Technology will offer plenty of options on new, bespoke sites. Indeed, considerable money has gone into attempts to use technology to resolve some of the issues discussed above. In some nations, all new large-scale infrastructure is designed with automation in mind. For instance, Saudi Arabia's ambitious $500 billion NEOM project – which includes a 170 km-long, car-free linear city – is not just futuristic in appearance; it was conceived from the ground up with integrated smart technologies, data-driven construction processes and modular elements that robotics can navigate. In Japan, where labour shortages are already acute, construction firms have embedded robotics systems into high-rise builds to provide precision design inputs needed to operate successfully. In both of these contexts, automation is integrated into the system's design, not awkwardly retrofitted into a legacy network.

Even so, we are still a long way from resolving the issues I've highlighted here. Construction robotics is a case in point: despite the huge investments poured into it, progress is highly constrained, especially in the UK, where such advances remain more concept than reality. For example, the SAM100 is one of the most advanced bricklaying robots available, designed for onsite masonry construction. SAM100 can lay around 3,000 bricks per day on ideal, flat surfaces. But it still requires human oversight, can't navigate uneven terrain or awkward corners and performs poorly in bad weather. On real-world sites, it simply can't replace a human crew.

What all this tells us is that skilled manual labour isn't just resistant to automation; it is fundamentally misaligned with AI's strengths. These jobs demand embodied intelligence, spatial reasoning, intuition and the ability to work through mess and variation. I'd argue that skilled work embodies some of the best examples of truly human work: complex, improvisational and grounded in physical reality.

The question of empathy

The other fundamentally human qualities that will prove important in the future are care and empathy. Some of the most resilient jobs of the AI age will be rooted in these qualities. Think of the nurse who calms a frightened patient at 2 a.m., not just administering medication but taking the time to listen to unspoken fears. Or the mental health counsellor who reads between the lines to recognise that what's not being said often speaks louder than what is. There are the childcare workers who navigate the chaotic emotional world of toddlers and carers for the elderly who manage not only physical tasks but also the delicate emotional terrain of dignity, loss and memory. These are all roles that demand emotional intelligence, something no algorithm has yet proved capable of convincingly imitating.

AI can simulate emotion, of course. Chatbots are already programmed to say things like 'I'm sorry you're feeling that way', or 'that must be difficult'. As anyone who has ever been on the receiving end of these platitudes knows, these are just lines and they ring hollow because of it. Trust is an emotional contract, and many people find it impossible to embrace machines in this way, especially in high-stakes, stressful contexts. A robot might successfully lift an elderly patient from a bed to a chair, but it cannot reassure her when she fears she's becoming a burden to her loved ones.

None of this means empathy-centred jobs won't evolve, or that AI won't take up more tasks. These things will happen. However, the core of caring and skilled professions, the part that involves one human being showing up fully for another or adapting in real time to a problem no one saw coming, currently remains out of AI's reach.

The future is hybrid

We need to be realistic: AI isn't static. It is evolving, and the commercial world recognises its real business value. Those firms that effectively leverage AI will reap the rewards. Any potential digital solution to make a professional sector more profitable and efficient will be considered; of that there is no doubt. We shouldn't rush to assume, though, that the outcome will always mean completely replacing what went before. Amid the urgency to understand what AI will replace, it's easy to overlook a more subtle, and arguably more transformative, development: roles in which humans don't compete against AI, but work with it.

The hybrid version of AI augments decisions rather than replacing human labour. Again, we're already seeing evidence of hybrid AI in action. Let's look at healthcare for an example. In Chapter 1, I pointed out how many roles in healthcare are being digitised; now, let's add some nuance to the situation, acknowledging that both humans and machines may have a place across many roles. For example, a doctor might use AI to scan radiology images and flag anomalies that a human operator looking through dozens of scans in a day might miss. Here, AI is not replacing the doctor's expertise, but expanding it.

Surgery offers another example. While robotic-assisted surgery has made great strides, human surgeons are still in the driving seat because they know how to interpret complex and often unpredictable variables that go beyond even the most sophisticated AI systems' real-time processing ability. Physiotherapy practitioners have the much-needed and very human ability to create an emotional rapport with patients, as well as picking up on and quickly adapting to subtle cues about pain or signs of discouragement or frustration. Paramedics, too, operate in environments where AI struggles. Arriving at the scene of a car crash, for example, they assess injuries, communicate with distressed victims and make split-second decisions. Sometimes they are required to comfort people in their final moments. It's impossible to replicate the experience and gut instinct it takes to triage under pressure or know when to bend protocol for the sake of a life.

This pattern occurs across professional sectors. In the field of law, language models are proving invaluable for rapidly drafting legal briefs or summarising case law, freeing time for human lawyers to do strategic thinking and engage more with clients. AI plays a similar role in the business setting, enabling executives to quickly analyse vast swaths of market data, converting seemingly chaotic input into the foundation for a coherent strategy. These are examples of humans and machines thinking together, each enhancing the other. While it is easy to be gloomy about the future of white-collar work, similar hybrid cooperation is occurring in almost every knowledge-based profession.

Skilled hybrid jobs

There are also countless examples of skilled workers using AI. Heat pump engineers, solar installers and EV technicians increasingly rely on AI-powered apps and digital systems to calibrate performance, monitor faults and log data. With smart systems embedded in everything from boilers to security setups, a modern tradesperson is just as likely to troubleshoot via tablet as spanner. In plumbing, AI-enhanced leak detection tools can analyse pressure patterns and flow data in real time. When it comes to electrical work, AI software is used to automatically flag safety risks before they become failures. Across the board, AI plays a role in ordering parts and managing inventory, automatically and seamlessly restocking raw materials while skilled workers are on the ground at job sites, saving time and reducing delays. AI-driven supply chain systems predict stock needs based on demand trends and seasonality. In construction, 3D scanning and modelling software, often powered by AI, helps visualise complex builds, foreseeing potential clashes in the schedule before they happen and optimising resource allocation. While an electrician might use AI-powered diagnostics to find wiring faults faster, fixing them still requires manual dexterity and situational judgement no algorithm can replicate. Likewise, a plumber may rely on AI to monitor flow data and predict leaks, but they still need to apply their wrench with judgement, adjusting to the environment they are in, whether they are knee-deep in damp insulation or battling with uneven pipes. Those human skills remain irreplaceable.

The basis for the success of each of these hybrid roles is similar to the one outlined in the previous section. AI is hugely sophisticated, but it can't do everything. It still needs judgement under uncertainty. It can provide options, probabilities and even recommendations, but it still struggles with ambiguity and context. Successful decision-making is more than choosing the best statistical option. A machine might advise a course of action based on pattern recognition, but a human must decide whether that action is moral, legal or desirable. The common thread is interpretation. Whether it's data, human values or appropriate responses, machines don't interpret; they compute, correlate and predict. Only humans can synthesise competing values, navigate ambiguity and accept responsibility for difficult trade-offs, and we are a way away from algorithms being able to carry those burdens alone.

AI needs humans to thrive

The hybrid future also isn't only about humans finding a way to fit into the new AI world of work; humans also have a crucial role in enabling AI to thrive. Behind nearly every autonomous system is an infrastructure of human labour. Our input is needed for everything from designing, training, auditing and maintaining models to supplying the energy and physical systems that make AI possible. In fact, some of the most urgent frontiers of human work lie in the ecological and material underpinnings of AI itself.

AI consumes vast amounts of energy. In 2024, data centres – including AI, crypto and general cloud services centres – accounted for around 415 terawatthours, or 1.5% of global electricity consumption. AI's energy consumption has grown 12% per year over the past five years and is projected to double by 2030.[12] The GPT-3 model was said to have consumed in the order of 1,300 megawatthours during its training run, roughly equivalent to the annual electricity use of 130 typical US homes.[13] A single ChatGPT-style query uses many times more energy than a simple web search. Google estimates that one Google search uses 0.3 watthours, compared to a ChatGPT request's 2.9 watthours.[14] Meanwhile, the power plants, substations, cooling infrastructure, grid interconnects and backup systems that power AI must be designed, built and managed, a process AI can assist with but not take over. It's also likely these skilled hybrid jobs will be highly localised, since it is impossible to offshore installation of a wind turbine in Essex to a data centre in Singapore. This infrastructure-level work will largely be done by local communities and managed by in-country experts.

Ideally, the expansion of AI will be done with one eye on the climate, leading to opportunities in solar panel installation, wind turbine maintenance, energy efficiency retrofits and grid modernisation. These jobs demand onsite judgement, improvisation and resilience in response to weather, terrain and regulatory complexities. An AI system might suggest optimal layouts, forecast energy yields, or monitor equipment status, but it cannot climb a turbine tower in a gale, rewire a misaligned cable in cramped space, or adapt to an unexpected equipment failure under tight timelines. Yes, AI's capabilities are expanding fast and change is coming. There are, however, opportunities to think about it in a positive way because in some circumstances it is bringing with it opportunity, at least for some who will work alongside it.

New kinds of AI-inspired jobs

A generation ago, no one aspired to be a UX designer because there were no smartphones. There were no cloud engineers, app developers or drone operators. No one was training to be a crypto analyst, meme strategist or VR therapist. These roles emerged because new technologies created new possibilities and, with them, new needs. The future of work is not static. It is organic, chaotic and endlessly generative. With its broad capacity to learn, simulate, automate and augment, AI is likely to spawn a huge number of jobs we can't even yet imagine because it doesn't just change what people do; it also changes how we define work, value and intelligence. It enables people to think, build and collaborate in previously unimaginable ways. In doing so, it will generate entire sectors of labour that feel as alien to us now as the job of 'influencer' would have to someone in 1985.

What might some of these new categories of work be? We can only speculate at this stage. We may see the rise of AI companionship coaches who help people navigate emotional relationships with AI beings. There may be a new breed of synthetic media editors, professionals trained to detect and validate content in a world of ubiquitous deepfakes and generative content. Entire professions may spring up around maintaining human dignity in AI-integrated care settings – perhaps empathy auditors, bias curators or algorithm ombudspeople. None of these titles are certain to develop, but all represent plausible responses to the pressures AI will bring.

The point here is not to predict these jobs with certainty. It's to understand that they will arrive, and when they do we must be ready to fill them. Retraining, for example, should not be treated as a stop-gap measure, a short course taken to patch a career after displacement, but framed as a permanent condition of working life in the AI age. Ultimately, the real winners will not just be those who hold on to old skills or fit neatly into today's growth sectors. They will be the ones who develop the skill of transition itself. They will be people willing to ask, again and again, 'What else can I become?'

Who is most at risk?

While much of this chapter has struck a note of optimism, we still can't escape the realities of the figures I opened it with: millions of people will lose their jobs, and far fewer people will find new opportunities or retrain and keep a place in the new order. Like so many previous seismic changes, the impact of AI will not be evenly spread across the world, or even in individual countries. It will deepen some divides, create new ones and reconfigure old hierarchies.

In some regions, AI offers a chance to leapfrog developmental bottlenecks by automating bureaucratic processes, improving access to healthcare and expanding digital education, and the benefits will improve the lives of many. In other regions, the potential outcomes are less positive, because AI may strip away the sources of economic advancement that globalisation once offered. Many developing nations, for example, mostly in the global south, have built significant employment sectors outsourcing white-collar labour, creating networks of call centres and basic coding, data entry and content moderation factories. These are the kinds of roles AI is poised to replace on an almost wholesale basis.

Regions heavily dependent on specific sectors face disproportionate risk. Cities built around legal services, accounting or administrative outsourcing may find themselves hollowed out by automation. The loss of great swathes of such jobs won't just affect individuals; it will strike at the fragile base of export-driven economies. When AI replaces a transcriptionist in Manila or a customer service rep in Nairobi, the revenue those workers once generated doesn't just disappear. It consolidates in AI-producing economies, deepening already-chronic global inequality. Since developing economies often lack the GDP or institutional capacity for rapid retraining, displaced workers within them face a precarious future. Worse, rural areas lacking high-speed internet or AI-relevant infrastructure could find themselves missing out on the economic upside altogether.

On the flip side, innovation hubs like Silicon Valley, London or Berlin may generate waves of new industries, further sharpening geographic inequality. Even in countries with such tech centres, economic benefits will accrue unevenly among communities. The data centres, proprietary models and capital investments that drive AI's development are increasingly controlled by a handful of mega-corporations. These firms can deploy AI to cut costs, optimise supply chains and dominate markets, creating enormous productivity gains, but those gains almost certainly won't trickle down to workers. They'll flow to shareholders, C-suite executives and highly specialised talent.

That's because the digital divide in advanced economies is not just about skills, but power, too. Workers at the bottom of the income ladder – often women, members of racial or ethnic minority groups, immigrants and younger employees – are more likely to hold precarious service jobs where AI is not always a positive development. 'Advances' like algorithmic scheduling in retail, automated productivity scoring in warehouses and AI-driven gig platforms can lock workers into unpredictable hours, erode bargaining power and intensify exploitation, all while generating data they have no ownership in.

The prognosis is not good, either, for those who go it alone. Large corporations are better positioned to withstand the huge shift than small and medium-sized enterprises (SMEs) because they have the capital, data infrastructure and in-house talent to integrate AI in strategic ways. SMEs, by contrast, are in a lose–lose position: they can adopt AI and risk displacing valued staff or fail to adopt and fall behind competitively. The latter scenario is the more likely, since most SMEs don't have access to proprietary models or AI engineers and are left relying on off-the-shelf solutions not be tailored to their needs.

Of course, nothing is yet set in stone, and the difference between disruption and devastation will be informed in large part by institutional response. Countries, regions or companies that invest in reskilling, digital literacy and AI design will find themselves better positioned to navigate this transition. Without intentional policy, investment in lifelong learning and mechanisms for broadly sharing AI's gains, however, even the wealthiest societies may find themselves more divided than ever.

THREE

AI Stagflation: Efficiency Without Prosperity

The great promise of digital technology has always been simple and seductive: each advance will improve life for everyone. It will create more output per worker and increase the wealth circulating through the economy, liberating us all to spend more time and energy on pursuits beyond mere survival. For much of recent history, that promise has broadly held true. The digital revolution that began in the late 20th century brought unprecedented efficiencies and new categories of work into existence. Sure, these great strides forward have not exactly spread the financial gains evenly, but most segments of society have seen at least some improvements. We no longer need to spend hours queueing at the bank to release our money or physically shop for the goods we need. We have rapid access to any information or media we want right at our fingertips. These are but a very few of the advantages digital technology brought us.

Now, though, we are entering uncharted territory. In the emerging age of AI, we can no longer assume that whatever comes next will continue to make our lives better. We've already reached the milestone at which intelligent systems can efficiently perform both repetitive labour and cognitive and creative tasks once thought to be uniquely performable by humans. This allows companies that have already taken advantage of AI developments to become leaner and more efficient while increasing productivity. *Leaner and more efficient* is, of course, business-speak for 'scaling down the workforce' – more bluntly, sacking people. Increasing numbers of firms are adopting these systems to help generate profit. Yet while the profit accumulates, it remains in the bank accounts of those who own the technology, while the humans who once built or created the same products and services with their labour are no longer required. As a result, the money these businesses generate is concentrated in fewer and fewer hands.

Confronting disruption

The impact of decoupling human input from productivity will be profound on many levels. Beyond impacting us personally, it will have grave large-scale consequences because it will usher in a future in which economic growth continues or even accelerates while overall prosperity falters or substantially declines for the vast majority of the population. Individual countries may register impressive GDP numbers fuelled by successful AI-powered enterprises while on the ground, millions experience unemployment. Those who manage to hang on to their positions will need to learn to live with the uncertainty of declining job security, falling wages and narrowing opportunities. Any money they have, they will be less likely to spend. The economic pie may grow, but fewer people will have a meaningful slice of it.

Industry disruption in any form is by nature uneven, throwing things out of whack. That's why we call it 'disruptive'. AI, though, creates disruption at a new order of magnitude. In industry shaped by AI, data and algorithm ownership will become the key fault line, and the tech barons who build the algorithms, own the platforms and, perhaps most crucially, hold the data, are in pole position to reap the lion's share of gains. The next big winners will be business owners who power their businesses using AI. However, a large percentage of the population – particularly those who rely on selling their labour to survive – will find that the future offers fewer assurances. Further, they will find it impossible to rely on the old labour model, where displaced workers retrained for new roles in adjacent industries. That's because AI isn't just disrupting one sector at a time; it's pervading nearly all of them simultaneously.

Stagflation, 1970s style

The current environment of progress without prosperity poses many dangers, including profound emotional, psychological and social impacts. It's not the only previously unknown threat we must contend with, though; AI stagflation will cause its own waves of disruption.

The term *stagflation* was coined in the 1970s to describe a toxic economic condition that orthodox models once insisted should not exist: high inflation combined with stagnant growth. For decades, economists had based their thinking around the assumption that inflation and unemployment always moved in opposite directions. If prices rose, growth and jobs should be strong. Conversely, if growth was weak, prices should remain stable. The oil crises of the 1970s shattered everyone's view of that neat relationship.

In 1973, crude oil prices tripled after the Organization of Petroleum Exporting Countries (OPEC) imposed an oil embargo in response to Western support for Israel during the Yom Kippur War. This unexpected backlash sent shockwaves through the industrial economies that had built their prosperity on cheap, abundant energy. Adding to the misery, a second shock hit in 1979, when the Iranian Revolution disrupted supplies, driving prices to new highs. Even before this, oil-importing countries like the UK found themselves grappling with a massive cost surge across the economy, which impacted every industry, including transport, heating and manufacturing. Even food production became more expensive. Inflation soared into double digits, eye-wateringly peaking at over 20% by the mid-1970s.

This was the time that proved all the economists' assumptions wrong. Higher prices did not translate into growth. Industries that relied on energy cut production, and many businesses struggling with rising costs slashed investment across the board. In the UK, the already-grave problem was compounded by a perfect storm of deep structural weaknesses. Even before the crisis, economic growth was blighted by low productivity, an ageing industrial infrastructure and the actions of powerful unions locked in a seemingly endless conflict with employers and government. The result was rising unemployment alongside spiralling prices: stagflation.

For ordinary people in the UK, the consequences of this period of stagflation were stark. Wages failed to keep pace with inflation, eroding living standards. Strikes spread across key industries, from coal mining to refuse collection, culminating in the Winter of Discontent from 1978 to 1979, when rubbish piled up in the streets and public services ground to a halt. For a while, the UK became the byword for *decline* in the eyes of the rest of the world. This once-great, productive nation was trapped in a cycle of inflation, stagnation and industrial strife. The inability of successive governments to resolve the crisis paved the way for Margaret Thatcher's election in 1979 and the shift towards monetarism, deregulation and curbs on union power. Even then, it took until the mid-1980s for the worst of the crisis to pass and oil prices to stabilise. Among the many lessons of this period is this: even the most confident economic model can rapidly unravel when the foundations of prosperity suddenly shift.

A new kind of stagflation

In the 1970s, it was energy that triggered the change. This was a resource everyone took for granted, but when it became a source of vulnerability, the fragility of building an economy on assumptions of endless supply was exposed. Today, we are facing a very different change in the foundations of prosperity that will bring massive economic change. This time though, the trigger won't be scarcity, but abundance. Intelligent machines promise relentless efficiency and ever-rising output, and the outcome has the potential to be just as destabilising to the economy as the 1970s energy crisis, if not more. In fact, the rise in the use of AI is creating a very real threat of stagflation in our own era. This new stagflation is not as black-and-white as the 1970s version, in which growth acted in inverse proportion with inflation. This time, we need to think about stagflation in a deeper, more structural sense, where economic gains are no longer tied to human advancement. Gains are still tied to growth and inflation, but the stakes are very different.

Let's start with growth. The big issue here is that growth will be impressive in the abstract but, for most of us, hollow in terms of lived reality. The tools of progress will widen the very divides they were once expected to close. AI may deliver the highest levels of productivity in human history, but without deliberate mechanisms to include most ordinary citizens in the benefits, that progress risks hardening into a condition of permanent imbalance. Productivity will rise, but few broad opportunities for prosperity will follow. Instead, the gains will accrue primarily to capital owners, concentrating wealth at the top. It doesn't matter if the system can produce more goods and services than ever before if the people who would consume have less purchasing power to do so. When workers become cut off from the gains of productivity, demand weakens. Consumption, the engine of most economies, will inevitably slow as wages stagnate or vanish altogether. Economic growth will falter even as output soars as all these AI-powered factories push out more goods at a faster rate. Without redistribution or new channels of income, there is a risk of a glut of production with insufficient buyers.

What, then, of the other half of this equation, inflation? Ironically, inflation can rise even in a world where technology delivers relentless efficiency. The problem lies not in scarcity, but in concentration. As firms consolidate around a handful of dominant AI platforms, the owners of those platforms will be able to dictate terms across multiple industries, extracting whatever software or hardware fees they please while keeping competitors at bay. Any business that wants to be part of the AI boom will have to pay whatever fees are asked, just as the cost of living surged in response to the demands of oil producers in the 1970s – because the world had no alternative. Adding to the imbalance, governments will face their own inflationary pressures, too. As more workers become displaced or deskilled, ruling parties from Westminster to Washington will be drawn into the role of guarantor, providing income support, retraining programmes or subsidies to maintain social stability. These interventions, however necessary, will expand public spending at the same time that tax revenues are shrinking, thanks to declining wage income. All these influences will combine to create *AI stagflation*, stagnant or uneven growth alongside pockets of inflation.

Though economists have not gone so far as to say this can't possibly happen, they have not spent much time making predictions or even talking about it. The comparisons are plain to see, however. The ruptures of the 1970s and the AI rupture we may be about to experience both undermine a deeply held belief about how economies function. In the 1970s, this belief was the faith that inflation and unemployment were inversely related. In the AI age, it is the belief that rising productivity will inevitably go on lifting living standards across the board, just as it has always done. If that link breaks, however, and growth can be measured but not felt by the wider world, what then?

The oil shocks that fuelled stagflation were sharp but resolved over a period of time as the politicians of the day overturned the Keynesian consensus. The changes they made were far-reaching, and it took a lot of pain before a resolution was reached, but eventually, they turned the situation around. In the current environment, however, there appear to be few options to do the same. The AI shock is set to be continuous and structural. We already know, with the advances we've seen, that AI's impact won't hit once and then fade, as the oil crisis did. It is already reshaping the way we live and work and will continue doing so indefinitely. What's more, the changes AI makes are global. No economy can insulate itself from algorithms and platforms that cross borders at the speed of data, and why would they? We're all still in thrall to the idea that technology will make our lives better and better. There is no doubt that a prolonged period of AI-driven dislocation will open the door to new economic ideologies. Whether these will be inclusive or exclusionary, stabilising or destabilising, will depend on how quickly societies recognise that the old assumptions no longer hold.

Learning from history: Japan

As successive governments look to clues from the history books when they finally begin to weigh policy responses, they might need to avoid the misleading example of Japan, frequently cited as an exemplary case of a highly industrialised nation integrating automation and robotics into its economy without triggering a wave of mass joblessness. Since the 1980s, Japanese firms have embraced robotics in manufacturing, service industries and even caring for the elderly. As this change developed, Japanese institutions built policies around job security and redeployment rather than widespread layoffs. Companies were encouraged to retrain their workers for new roles, supported by a culture that valued long-term employment. Meanwhile, the government invested heavily in technical education and vocational training, ensuring workers could adapt to changing demands.

As a result of these policy decisions, Japan became one of the most automated nations in the world while also maintaining comparatively low unemployment. There was, however, a downside: Japan succeeded in preserving jobs, but it didn't energise growth or stimulate broad-based economic prosperity at the same time. Workers were not thrown out of the system, but they were also not pulled upward by it. Many became trapped in roles with little wage progression or innovation. *Underemployment*, where workers remain employed but in roles beneath their potential, became widespread. Though the steps the Japanese government took ensured employment was protected, it was unable to leverage productivity growth – or, indeed, consumption – to the maximum.

The result of all of this was economic stagnation. The collapse of Japan's asset bubble in the early 1990s led to what has become known as its 'lost decades'. During this time, the country experienced prolonged deflation, low GDP growth and flat or declining wages. Even after all the protective measures taken, job security was eventually under threat, too, with growing numbers of short-term (read: *precarious*) employment contracts. Japan's approach does tell us something useful, though, and that is that maintaining steady levels of employment is not the same as ensuring economic vitality. While the country did an admirable job maintaining social cohesion and avoiding crisis at a time of change, it did so at the expense of its long-term economic strength.

A self-perpetuating problem

The challenge in solving AI stagflation is that it will reinforce itself. Each wave of automation increases efficiency within firms but reduces the aggregate demand that drives the wider economy. Productivity gains will accrue in narrow pockets – mostly those of the few companies that build or own AI infrastructure – while wages, consumption and investment lag behind. At the same time, the financial system will amplify this imbalance. It is inevitable that investors will pour capital into AI ventures, speculating on future dominance rather than immediate productivity. The result will be asset inflation rather than real economic growth, a typical 'bubble', except this time, the underlying technology is genuinely transformative. It's a paradox that even genuine innovation can stall an economy if its benefits are too concentrated, returns too delayed or social effects too disruptive. The more AI promises, the more it risks distorting the balance between investment and output, or, in other words, between what the economy can do and what people can afford to consume.

In this climate, central banks may find themselves in an impossible trap. Raising interest rates to curb inflation, for example, could choke investment in struggling sectors, exacerbating an already-desperate unemployment situation. Yet loosening policy to stimulate demand could risk further emboldening the handful of monopolistic firms and intensifying fiscal imbalances. Even well-intentioned policy interventions, such as introducing tax incentives to encourage firms to hire more workers, will struggle to gain traction. The economy will be too volatile.

It won't help, either, that policy-makers won't have the full picture. AI tools often improve performance in ways that don't show up in national accounts, such as improving workflows or ensuring fewer errors. Until these micro-level efficiencies aggregate into macro-level output, they'll remain invisible to the economy's metrics and, crucially, to confidence. Policy-makers will find themselves trying to manage a ghost economy that feels more productive but doesn't pay more or grow faster.

As we've discussed, at its core, AI stagflation is not a story of an economic cycle waiting to turn. It will be a globally transformative change that will unfold unevenly. We've never seen anything like it before, which makes it very difficult to come up with a policy response that will mitigate its impact. That said, in the next chapter, we will try.

FOUR

Policy Levers In The AI Era

It would not be unreasonable to expect that someone in a position of power is working to manage the radical changes we are already experiencing and plan for the threat of AI stagflation. At the very least, there should be processes in place to guide and shape the machines, interpreting their output and ensuring they behave ethically and safely. When a self-driving car glitches and causes accidents or a predictive policing algorithm shows racial discrimination or a hiring AI turns out to have a gender bias, there must be a way to investigate and hold systems accountable.

As AI systems begin to influence everything from education policy to criminal justice to welfare eligibility, government institutions and non-governmental organisations (NGOs) need to evolve in real time so they can act as effective custodians of the AI ecosystem, overseeing its implementation and enforcing its boundaries. People in multiple roles will have to get involved – including civil servants, policy analysts, technologists, legal scholars and ethicists – because it will be a huge undertaking to ensure AI is deployed in alignment with democratic principles, public interest and human dignity. Such work will require deep institutional knowledge, political sensitivity and an understanding of both technological systems and human rights frameworks.

Waiting for policy

Unfortunately, the clear message here is, *Don't hold your breath waiting for policies to ease an undoubtedly painful transition.* Our systems of power and administration are already overwhelmed by the speed and scale of the changes they've seen unleashed on their watch. Governments, corporations and public institutions that are supposedly designed to manage complex issues are trapped in a structural mismatch: their processes move at the snail's pace, while technology evolves at a breathtaking speed.

Policy-makers are facing an almost impossible dilemma. We, the electors, expect them to be both stable and responsive, but they somehow also need to juggle the processes of deliberation, consultation and regulation while keeping up with technologies that reinvent themselves every few months. What is exasperating is that these policy-makers don't seem to be making the effort to work out a middle ground. As a result, we're living in a world paralysed by process. Policy cycles stubbornly continue to run on timelines measured in years. A typical parliamentary inquiry into an emerging technology almost always lasts longer than the product's entire life cycle. Even when governments appear to have the desire to act relatively swiftly, bureaucracy inevitably steps in the way of progress.

AI touches all aspects of our lives, which means that multiple overlapping departments have a role in pronouncing on policy, and each one has its own consultation requirements. A single initiative to oversee one aspect of AI must often pass through years of pilot phases, audits and interdepartmental approvals before deployment. By the time regulation is debated, drafted and implemented, the underlying technology has already mutated or become obsolete after being disrupted by an entirely different technology.

The policy–technology gap

It doesn't help that there is a communication gap between policy-makers and technologists. Those writing the regulations often don't understand the underlying technologies, adding to the challenge of working out the best way to govern AI platforms and online services. That's even before policy-makers begin looking for aspects of the technology that are potentially unethical or damaging in the long term, so bad actors can be reined in before things go wrong. The machinery of government is trying to oversee tools it doesn't fully understand, using processes that can't move fast enough to make any difference.

There is, however, an urgent need for institutional involvement. Those building and funding AI technology have thus far shown little appetite to consider the potentially negative impacts of using their creations. Without any obvious moves to check their progress, technology firms can continue unhindered by any sort of accountability. Meanwhile, the longer policy-makers do nothing, the chances of being able to course-correct at some point down the line become more and more unlikely. AI, automation and data systems evolve on cycles measured in weeks, sometimes just days. Meanwhile, governments and regulators function on cycles measured in years or electoral terms. The ever-widening gap between policy and technology is the fault line of the 21st century. Today, technological capability races ahead while social, ethical and political adaptations remain virtually stationary.

The underlying cause of institutional inaction is structural, as institutions have been built around linear change. Our political systems are rooted in a world where cause and effect unfold slowly enough that there's time to study, deliberate about the impact and respond accordingly. Yet AI's impact is nonlinear. A small capability gain today can trigger cascading effects across entire industries or societies tomorrow. Traditional governance mechanisms – such as consultation papers, impact assessments and pilot schemes – have no chance in keeping up. By the time the regulatory machinery grinds into action to begin its initial analysis, the ground has shifted again. The negative impact of this time lag is compounded by a deeper philosophical gap. Our systems are built on the assumption that the world can be measured, mapped and managed through rational planning. However, in the AI era, this assumption holds us back. AI introduces forms of complexity that are not just unknown, but unknowable. Machine learning models generate correlations that even their creators can't always fully explain.

The ever-widening space between policy and technological development is more than just an administrative inconvenience. It creates *policy distortion,* in which efforts to catch up amplify the very problems they were meant to solve. Governments get stuck on attempts to regulate already-outdated technologies while ignoring emerging ones. This, in turn, erodes trust. Voters lose confidence in governments that always seem surprised by crises, whether economic, environmental or technological. The longer this persists, the greater the temptation to bypass institutions altogether will become. People are already turning to technology companies for services that governments can't deliver and looking to algorithms for the authority leaders no longer appear to have. The danger is not so much that institutions fail, but that they quietly become irrelevant.

Waiting is not an option

We can only speculate what happens next. Right now, it seems likely that private systems will increasingly assume the function of our public institutions. Algorithms could decide who receives credit, healthcare, education or visibility, while private platforms may mediate everything from news to democratic participation. What began as institutional lag could end as institutional outsourcing, where public purpose is defined not by deliberation, but by data.

Whatever the future may bring, without a doubt, the time to act is now. It is arguably already too late, but continuing to do nothing is no longer an option. The challenges of the AI era will be reengineering bureaucracy and building institutions capable of continuous learning, smart decision-making and adaptive regulation. Ironically, that may well mean borrowing from the very systems AI seeks to govern so the process of regulation becomes decentralised, data-driven and iterative. Until this happens, our governments and institutions will fall further and further behind.

When laws and basic governance lag so far behind innovation, they leave us open to threats on our livelihoods and living standards. Without policy interventions, we may be left exposed to systems we cannot see and decisions we cannot contest. The politicians and institutions that should be there to protect us instead could pave the way for widening inequality as those with access to tools, data and insight pull ever further ahead, while the majority are left behind. As a result, a handful of mega-corporations could set the rules, determining the terms that the dwindling workforce are hired on. As a result, at a societal level, the gap between people and power would deepen, eroding trust and deepening disengagement, which could well result in further grave consequences.

Performative regulation

Aside from being woefully behind the times, there's another, perhaps even less palatable reason why our politicians are slow to respond to perceived threats from AI. It's a scenario as old as politics itself: it is simply not seen as politically expedient to stand in the way of potential gains from technology. There are plenty of upsides to AI, too, and no government wants to appear anti-innovation. This is why any regulation we do see on the technology is mostly performative. It's drafted, redrafted, endlessly consulted on, then quietly watered down or delayed. For example, the European Union's AI Act, which came into force in August 2024, is comprehensive in scope, but critics point out ample built-in opportunities to soften or delay many of its provisions, noting that many of the provisions already lag behind technology updates.[15]

That same pattern is already playing out in the UK. The government has repeatedly stated its aim to make Britain a global AI hub, which does much to explain its hesitant regulatory posture. While successive governments have generated multiple discussion papers, statements of ethical principles and voluntary codes of conduct, as yet no binding framework with enforcement teeth has been produced. Westminster's tone seems deliberately soft, built around buzzy terms like *pro-innovation* and *light touch*. Of course, the biggest incentive to do nothing to impede AI's progress in the UK and elsewhere is the fact that AI is borderless. Its dataset models and applications cross jurisdictions instantly. Political leaders across the globe recognise its strength as a geopolitical asset, and no state wants to handicap its own champions. The potential to lose billions in investment funds to more permissive jurisdictions no doubt keeps UK ministers awake at night.

Each jurisdiction has a slightly different approach to technology, reflecting the political DNA of the country that made it. The United States, for example, emphasises innovation and competition, while the European Union high-lights precaution and human rights and China is 100% state-controlled and directed. These different approaches decrease the likelihood that concrete efforts will be undertaken to regulate or manage AI. This absence of global coordination creates a regulatory vacuum. Building AI technology might be billed as a race to the top, but the reality is that it is a race to the bottom. Every country is claiming leadership, but none is ready to provide stewardship.

Without clear rules or a global agreement, tech companies will inevitably exploit the ambiguity, releasing products faster than they can properly test or understand them. The danger is not simply that some tools will malfunction, but that the global culture of innovation will normalise recklessness. Without enforceable standards, competition between tech giants will become a race to the edge. They will want to launch first and scale fastest, and if anything doesn't quite go as planned, they will apologise later. The pressure to dominate markets will drive companies to deploy powerful systems into education, health, finance and media before their risks are fully known or understood. If people are harmed, well, that becomes data for the next update – and data is, of course, what counts.

The threat of data capitalism

The failure of governments across the world leaves us vulnerable to *data capitalism*, in which information, arguably the most valuable resource in the world, is privately owned, endlessly extracted and largely ungoverned. A concentration of power around data would completely reshape the balance between public and private authority. Today, a small cluster of firms can do what entire industries and governments cannot: process data at a planetary-scale, train trillion-parameter models and deploy them globally within days. In practical terms, the cost of entry into frontier AI development is prohibitive for all but a few companies. Training a single state-of-the-art model like the latest iteration of ChatGPT or Google's Gemini costs tens or even hundreds of millions. This concentration of investment ultimately creates an unshakeable monopoly. The companies with the most users have the most data. The more data they have, the better their models become. The better their models, the more users they attract. Each cycle tightens the grip, ensuring no one else has a chance to enter and compete on the market, no matter how innovative their idea.

For governments, this power asymmetry poses a profound challenge. When a small number of companies become essential to national economies, critical infrastructure and even military applications, regulation is impossible. No state can afford to alienate the firms that operate its economic backbone. The negative consequences of this are profound. The power asymmetry will deepen economic inequality, since AI's productivity gains will first flow to those with access to data and computing power. The firms at the top will have carte blanche to extract disproportionate returns, while workers and smaller businesses experience pressures on wages, profit margins and autonomy. There's also a democratic dimension to this power concentration. In previous eras, states controlled the processes that distributed information, from postal systems to broadcast licences. Today, private platforms govern the informational environment that shapes public opinion, civic trust and even electoral outcomes. The same systems that can compose poetry or write software can also easily manufacture misinformation, manipulate attention and subtly shape behaviour.

Multiple stories have already circulated of AI being used in controversial ways, such as predicting the likelihood of criminal re-offence, distributing social benefits or allocating precious resources. Each of these deployments raises fundamental questions. Who gets to decide which data is used? How do we ensure due process in decisions made by machines? How do we create transparency in systems that few people understand? These are civic questions, not engineering problems, and they require a new generation of public servants and civic leaders to tackle them. When governments delay or water down regulation, they effectively delegate power to whoever moves fastest. Today, a handful of corporations have been empowered to set the rules of the digital economy, giving a small number of unelected – and unaccountable – CEOs the power to determine what is possible, permissible and profitable.

Three imperfect solutions

Politicians from both sides of the political spectrum will no doubt try to assure us they are on top of things. 'We can control it,' they will say. 'We can mitigate any impact.' Such overconfidence in expertise is one of modern history's most recurring delusions. In the mid-20th century, for example, leading economists including

John Maynard Keynes and policy-makers such as US President John F. Kennedy and UK Prime Minister Harold Macmillan began to talk about the 'end of boom-and-bust'. They believed that with the right monetary tools and fiscal management, the violent cycles that had shaped capitalism since the Industrial Revolution could be smoothed out, even eliminated. For a time, it looked convincing, too. The post-war economies grew steadily, inflation seemed manageable and recessions were relatively shallow.

The hubris behind this attitude, however, was brutally exposed in 2008, when the entire world financial system teetered on the brink of collapse. At the heart of the issue were highly trained experts who had designed complex instruments that they insisted were safe. Two prime examples would be mortgage-backed securities and collateralised debt obligations, which bundled large number of home loans, including high risk subprime mortgages into products that were sold to investors as if they were relatively safe. When borrowers began to default at scale, the true risk embedded into these complex, opaque instruments were exposed, triggering massive losses in the financial system. Regulators had taken their eye off the ball, believing they had the tools to contain systemic risk while still reassuring the public that modern finance had evolved beyond the volatility of the past. In a matter of weeks in March 2008, the markets imploded, economies contracted and millions lost jobs and homes. So much for controlling the cycle of boom-and-bust.

Our current situation has some worrying parallels with the 2008 financial crisis. Just as economists and financiers once believed they could model away risk, many technologists and policy-makers today express faith that AI can be safely managed and contained within existing frameworks. They assume that regulation, oversight and technical safeguards will be enough to keep systems aligned with human intent, working towards our best interests. Yet this confidence is, at best, naive or misplaced and, at worst, downright negligent. Many of the tech giants leading the race to embrace AI are adept at deflecting scrutiny on their algorithms, and the ruling parties are complicit, not asking too many questions of the powerful coterie of billionaire tech bros. If history teaches anything, it is that claims of control at moments of profound transition should be treated with deep scepticism.

Let's say, however, that governments decide doing nothing is not an option. What policy levers do they have at their disposal? The options most likely to be considered fall into three broad camps: regulatory, redistributive and adaptive. Sadly, none of these options is straightforward, and each comes with trade-offs of its own that make its success far from guaranteed. Let's look at each one in more detail.

1. Regulation

The longest shot, in my view, would be to seek to break up or regulate dominant AI firms in the hope of restoring competition and preventing excess concentration of pricing power. The rationale behind this idea is clear: concentrated market power distorts pricing, weakens innovation and suppresses income shares for workers. It also allows a small cluster of firms to accumulate vast control over data, infrastructure and digital markets.

While the logic of stepping in with regulations is compelling, this approach's potential to succeed is next to zero. The billionaires behind the big AI firms have already demonstrated how powerful they are. When they meet with prime ministers and presidents around the world, there is no doubt about who is calling the shots. For instance, for a short while, Elon Musk – the head of SpaceX, Tesla and X and the wealthiest person in human history – even took up a prime position in US President Donald Trump's second administration.

For the sake of clarity, let's play out the regulatory solution. The first barrier to acknowledge is the fundamental mismatch between national regulatory frameworks and globalised tech platforms. Each of the dominant AI companies – whether developing foundational models, controlling massive computer infrastructure or aggregating global datasets – effortlessly operates across borders. This means that they have customers in dozens of countries, serve billions of users and – just to remain neutral, you understand – hold subsidiaries in favourable tax and legal jurisdictions. Therefore their operations, assets and influence are dispersed across the globe, while the regulatory tools designed to govern them remain anchored to individual jurisdictions.

This asymmetry paves the way for a constant game of jurisdictional arbitrage. If a country tightens antitrust rules, raises corporate taxes or even debates enforcing data protection laws, AI firms can swiftly shift operations elsewhere, creating a threat of economic or strategic retaliation against regulation. Since these firms have already proved to be key drivers of national tech ecosystems by creating jobs, fuelling exports and offering strategic AI capabilities, governments knuckle down pretty quickly in response to the threat. The incentive for countries to compete for AI firms' favour rather than confront them is baked into the relationship.

We've already seen evidence of this dynamic in successive attempts to create a global corporate tax system. Governments around the world have been trying for more than a decade to close tax loopholes that allow multinational tech firms to shift profits to low-tax jurisdictions like Ireland, the Netherlands or Bermuda. Firms such as Apple, Google and Meta have legally funnelled billions in global profits through these jurisdictions, paying effective tax rates that are dramatically lower than those domestic companies pay. Despite widespread public condemnation and protracted international negotiations, progress on this issue has been somewhere between painstakingly slow and almost non-existent. Even when they are hit with massive fines following successive anti-trust actions, tech firms appear to see such penalties as the cost of doing business rather than existential threats. All this raises the question, if international regulators couldn't coordinate effectively on something as universally measurable as corporate tax, how likely are they to succeed in dismantling AI monopolies?

An alternative solution, breaking big tech's stranglehold by subsidising a legion of new competitors, is not a plausible option either. These tech giants have already been around for a good while and built themselves a firm foothold, including, crucially, extensive data ecosystems and developer networks. As a result, the big AI firms have huge user bases that reinforce their power. The more users a platform has, the more data it gathers. The more data it gathers, the better its models perform. The better its models, the more users it attracts. This self-reinforcing system is almost impossible to break, as the situation currently stands. Any new competitors governments subsidised would have substantially poorer capabilities, leaving them in a weakened position to compete with established tech giants.

Despite the difficulties, what we are seeing now from global governments is tacit regulatory surrender. Governments may criticise tech giants in public, but behind closed doors they lay out the red carpet. Political regimes don't consider trying to weaken their tech champions because it would give geopolitical rivals an edge.

2. Redistribution

If direct regulation of AI monopolies is the longest shot, how about profit redistribution? The idea is to take some of the extraordinary profits generated by AI and channel them back into the broader economy through universal basic income (UBI), wage subsidies or large-scale retraining programmes. This would keep consumer demand alive even as traditional employment contracts shrink while ensuring that displaced workers maintain purchasing power, thus stabilising the demand shortfall that drives stagnation.

Like regulation, the redistribution approach has much to recommend it, and on its face, it looks like a straightforward and fair system. In this case, AI productivity gains would be treated as a form of collective wealth. This could be seen as tacit acknowledgement that all AI's algorithms, datasets and digital infrastructure were built through our collective contribution via the human-generated data that feeds machine learning. From this perspective, redistribution could be seen as a dividend on shared human contribution.

In practice, though, redistribution on this scale faces as many hurdles as regulation. It is highly unlikely the major tech firms will be keen to put their hands in their pockets for this sort of deal. The failure of global taxation initiatives shows the extent of multinationals' resistance to sharing their gains, and individual countries have no lobbying power with these organisations. If governments struggle to enforce even modest tax reforms, how likely are they to extract sustained streams of revenue from the world's most profitable AI firms? It is highly unlikely that individual governments could put a redistribution system together by themselves. Redistribution requires sustained public finance at a time when many governments are already heavily indebted. In the wake of the COVID-19 pandemic, many advanced economies carry debt-to-GDP ratios above 100%, while developing countries are in even more significant debt distress. The idea that a state could suddenly fund permanent UBI or massive retraining schemes seems implausible, even before we consider that governments' traditional payroll tax revenue is being eroded by automation.

Some economists have proposed automation taxes or data dividends for large firms that switch to AI or automation. The logic here is that if a business pays payroll tax on human workers, it should also pay when it replaces those workers with AI systems. Building a political consensus for this type of radical redistribution, however, would be very difficult. Wealthy corporations are adept at lobbying, shaping narratives and structuring finances to minimise liabilities. It's very likely that proposals for UBI would be framed among these entities as radical socialism or social welfare and quickly killed off through partisan politics. In most countries, the chances of systemic reform of this type are about the same as regulatory limits on the power of AI giants.

3. Adaptation

The final option is to do what humans have always done: adapt. Every great technological wave from the Industrial Revolution to the computer age has been turbulent, but all eventually generated more jobs than they destroyed. The optimistic point of view is that AI, despite its unprecedented scope, may follow the same pattern. To realise this, however, we'd need to be in a position where AI not only automated existing roles, but also created new domains of human endeavour. Think of the rise of car ownership, which spawned all sorts of new jobs, such as mechanics, highway engineers and even property developers, who built new houses for people who no longer needed to live within walking distance of work. In the same way, AI might spark demand for specialists in data ethics, human–AI collaborative design, synthetic biology or industries we can scarcely imagine today.

The most obvious riposte to this rosy argument is that of scale. Even if entirely new categories of work do emerge, is it realistic to imagine they can absorb the millions of workers displaced from traditional employment? The risk is that adaptation will benefit only a small, elite group while the broader population lags behind. For every high-paid AI ethicist or human-centred AI designer, how many factory workers or clerical staff will struggle to transition into roles requiring radically different aptitudes? The large number of deprived areas in the UK following the factory closures of the 1970s and 1980s bear testimony to the likelihood of this outcome.

The other big challenge is timing. In the past, transitions from one economic regime to another have unfolded over decades, even generations. It took almost a century for labour markets to stabilise after the first mechanised looms. Arguably, we are still working through the fallout from the digital transition, which forced so many out of work. By contrast, AI is advancing at a breakneck pace, compressing cycles of innovation into years rather than decades. There is a fear that any new roles won't just be inadequate in number, but may also arrive too slowly, leaving a prolonged dislocation gap in which unemployment, underemployment and social unrest dominate. In principle, adaptation may appear the most sustainable path among the three solutions because it builds new sources of work, rather than compensating for work's absence. Yet in practice, adaptation is a race against time, and even if there is some success, the results will be patchy.

No single solution to the coming AI crisis looks wholly adequate. Regulation appears highly unlikely and redistribution would be equally politically fragile. Meanwhile, adaptation is uncertain in scope and timing. The most likely outcome is a patchwork of partial solutions unevenly applied across countries, which may or may not mitigate some of the pain. The real question is not whether AI's negative impacts can be 'solved', but whether societies can endure and manage them long enough for new equilibria to emerge.

FIVE

The Age Of Dislocation: The Human Cost Of Transformation

Work has always been a source of structure in our lives. You may never have thought about it in this way, but our jobs act as the invisible scaffolding that organises our time, relationships and identity. They dictate when we wake, where we go, what we wear and who we see. Take them away, and the day loses its shape. This is a big reason why many people find it so hard to adjust to retirement. Joblessness impacts us more beyond making us feel our days aren't very organised, though. Western culture equates productivity with virtue, making the absence of work feels like moral failure. That mindset can do some real mental and physical harm. Long-term unemployment has been linked with depression, social withdrawal, poorer physical health and lower self-esteem. Since large-scale job losses are predicted, thanks to AI, we need to consider the human toll of what comes next.

The coming human identity crisis

There is no doubt that the rise of artificial intelligence will have an outsize impact on society. It wouldn't be an exaggeration to suggest the change is highly likely to result in a crisis of identity. I call it a 'crisis' because, for many people, unemployment may turn out to be a permanent state of affairs. In the past, losing a job may have been put down to bad luck or economic downturn, and jobs were generally cyclical, so recoverable. In extreme cases, a person may have needed to retrain for a different profession, but in time things would improve.

There will be no such certainties in the AI era. Some people may never even get onto the first rung of the job ladder, and among those who do, any job loss could well spell the end of their career. There is no certainty that the same technology that automates one role will create another of equal value. Under these circumstances, reskilling, once the default remedy to redundancy, will be like running up a down escalator, since the faster workers adapt, the faster the system will change.

The notion of a career as a life story told through the language of progression depends on continuity. When that continuity breaks, so does the sense of self built around it. The years of effort, training and sacrifice that once pointed toward a stable future suddenly grind to a halt. The psychological disorientation of permanent unemployment will be profound. Imagine how sobering it would be to realise that no amount of initiative or loyalty can restore your place in the world. Next, you might think that losing your job feels like a verdict on your relevance. That's because the underlying message is, *Your kind of work no longer matters.*

We already know that changes to the job market will impact those in the knowledge economy first. Very often, these professions are extremely intertwined with personal identity because they are built on title and status. When AI replaces a designer, journalist or analyst, the loss feels personal for them, an indictment of that promise that we can 'be anything' if we work hard enough. Technology will destroy the age-old promise of the meritocracy, and the question will become, *What happens to self-worth in a world where effort and outcome are no longer correlated?*

When algorithms become colleagues

What, then, of those who manage to hang on to their jobs? In recent years, the workplace has changed irrevocably, and there are many more changes to come. If the axe does not fall straight away, those in work will find themselves increasingly looking over their shoulders, wondering whether the skills they built their lives around will soon be automated. Even if their jobs feel secure, at least for now, many may find themselves feeling hollowed out as their day-to-day tasks become less creative and increasingly geared toward algorithm supervision. We are told that AI will make us more efficient and improve our output, yet each breakthrough tightens the loop of uncertainty, raising even more questions about purpose and control. The more that parts of our roles are outsourced to machines, the less confidence we will have in our own judgement. The pressure will be enormous. Every update, tool or new skill demanded in our evolving workplace will feel like a test of relevance. We will bear the brunt of the struggle to stay current, and any success will feel temporary.

There is a cognitive dissonance around progress that also reflects a deeper truth about AI. We are innovating faster than we can integrate these innovations into our day-to-day working life. While technology evolves exponentially, capability and understanding evolve on a linear level. The result is a widening gap between what we know how to do and what we can quickly adapt to. Even when we understand the brief, it's exhausting living alongside systems that demand constant adaptation and, indeed, unwavering attention. Every notification, feed and prompt is a small intrusion into our working day, breaking our focus and subtly eroding our sense of control. AI promises seamless connectivity, but it can behave as a series of endless interruptions in one form or another. The workers of the future may face the impossible task of keeping pace with a machine that never sleeps.

This type of work could also have a psychological cost that may shift the way we behave in the workplace. For example, workers may become more cautious and deferential, afraid to challenge systems that could easily replace them, and this quiet fear may seep into the culture of workplaces, discouraging risk-taking. There might be other sources of pressure, too. The rules of supply and demand mean the pendulum of power could swing firmly towards business owners who can pick and choose their workforce. They will, of course, only want the best, hardest workers who put in maximum performance every day, and they'll want to use the best tool just to be sure they have them.

There is already increasing use of new, AI-based forms of surveillance and assessment, billed as tools to increase efficiency. Don't underestimate the potential negative impacts they could have on employee well-being, however, when algorithms constantly monitoring productivity, sentiment and even tone of voice. When trust between employer and employee is mediated by data, their sense of a human relationship disappears.

Democracies depend on a shared belief in process. This is the foundation of our trust in the legitimacy of our institutions, the reliability of their information and the fairness of our systems. If these foundations erode in the AI era, suspicion and resentment will proliferate.

A new generational divide

At the beginning of this book, I referred to the social contract that we once took for granted: that our lives would be better than our parents', and the lives of our children would be better than ours. Those presumed certainties are now gone. They've been replaced by an ominous generational divide, which is bad for everyone, whatever their age. AI is rewriting the rules, creating stark differences between the experiences and expectations of both young and old, neither one positive. This may seem like an acute generalisation, but for clarity, the older generation I'm referring to contains those whose lives and careers to date were shaped by institutions that promised perhaps not jobs for life, but certainly lifelong careers with mostly predictable progress. In this context, the younger generation contains those who may not yet have started their first job and may, indeed, never experience what it is like to take part in the working world.

For many older workers, the pace of technological transformation has been relentless. This cohort has had to adapt to a new digital world of tools, interfaces and expectations that seem to change faster than they can be mastered. The familiar landscapes of the workplace have been upended, as have the norms they once relied on, such as skill mastery and workplace seniority improving with age. Adaptability has become the defining skill for this generation. Workers who trained for one career now, if they are lucky, pursue several, perpetually retraining to stay relevant in an economy that no longer rewards loyalty but rewards agility instead. Experience, once the mark of authority, is no longer valued as an asset.

The younger cohort is having a very different, but equally disorienting, experience. They are the so-called *digital natives*, the first generation to grow up with a screen in-hand and a networked world as the default environment. They are adept at moving fluidly through technologies that bewilder their elders, intuitively adapting to platforms and tools that shift overnight. To them, technological change is not a disruption but a condition of existence. Yet this fluency carries its own cost: instability is the only stability they have ever known. Many of this generation are growing up with the sense that they are preparing for jobs that may vanish before they reach them. From childhood, they have lived in a permanent state of performance, carefully curating their identities online and preparing to navigate a precarious job market increasingly characterised by automation, short-term contracts and algorithmic hiring systems. Being talented or qualified is no longer a golden ticket. Further, generative AI has blurred the line between human creativity and machine output, forcing many young people to ask a question no previous generation faced: what does it mean to be 'good at something' when a machine can do it faster, cheaper and, often, convincingly enough?

For all their differences, however, both generations share common emotional ground in their fear for the future. Both see that something foundational is slipping away. For the older generation, it is the stability that once anchored effort to reward. For the younger generation, it is the assurance that effort leads anywhere at all. That's just about all they have in common though, and their differences continuously widen the empathy gap between them. The older generation views the younger as restless, entitled and impatient, unwilling to pay their dues in a world that still, the older generation believes, rewards diligence. The younger generation, in turn, see their elders as rigid, complacent and complicit. *Things were so much easier in the olden days, they think.* They are resentful, too, that the previous generations were responsible for building the systems that now fail to include them. In other words, each group sees the other's struggle as self-inflicted.

It is easy to make such assumptions amid the deep-rooted changes we are now experiencing, but in fact, both generations are trapped in the logic of their time. The older generations were shaped by institutions that promised permanence, and they are bewildered by those institutions' collapse, while the younger generations were born into flux and have never known anything else. Both, quite rightly, feel powerless to change what is happening. Divides like the one between generations chip away at the cohesion of society. Communities hold together because they trust that progress connects them and moves everyone towards something better. When that trust erodes, resentment floods in, and the very idea of a better future changes from a common target to a contested resource. The danger is that, without the potential for progress, the generational divide is another step towards things falling apart.

Leaving people behind

When societies resist the march of progress, their reactions tend to follow a familiar pattern. After a period of denial, during which communities cling to old certainties and insist the change is only temporary, they experience anger and resistance. In the early years of the Industrial Revolution, for example, the Luddite uprisings saw looms and frames systematically smashed not, as is sometimes portrayed, in a blind rage against technology, but as a desperate protest against unemployment, wage cuts and erosion of livelihoods. Similarly, in the 1980s, globalisation, cheaper overseas labour and automation hollowed out miners' livelihoods, sparking the miners' strike of 1984 to 1985. The strike spilled over into pitched battles between strikers and police, fuelled by frustrations at deepening poverty and a feeling among whole communities that they had been abandoned by Westminster.

Is this what we should expect when the true impact of AI fully sinks into widespread consciousness? According to current projections, hundreds of thousands – perhaps millions – could see their livelihoods swept away by automation within a few short years. Jobs that once provided stability and identity, from clerical roles to creative professions, will almost certainly disappear faster than new opportunities appear. For individuals in those jobs, the challenge is not only financial but existential. Without purpose, wages or hope, these people could lose faith in the system – or even society itself.

If AI disrupts service and knowledge work at scale, as is predicted, the consequences could be just as destabilising as the previous major economic shifts, if not more. The difference is that, this time, change would not be concentrated in coal towns or industrial centres, but spread across professional classes that have long considered themselves insulated from such shocks. This, in turn, could result in falling consumer spending, which would weaken businesses and hollow out communities as young people leave in search of work, and public services would be strained under the weight of rising inequality. The transition to an AI-driven economy may ultimately create extraordinary wealth, but most likely only for a small proportion of society, leaving behind the vast majority.

Civic erosion

Inevitably, when such large groups of workers feel abandoned, the consequences reach far beyond the labour market. In the case of AI, they appear set to reshape the civic foundations of the country in ways we're only beginning to understand. We know that when people feel abandoned by opportunity and policy, there is growing mistrust of the political system that seems to have largely written them off, or at least, does nothing to improve the situation. In towns like Blackpool, Middlesbrough and Stoke-on-Trent, for example – at the centre of regions marked by long-term industrial decline, where jobless numbers are high – voter turnout is consistently lower than the national average, often by a long way.[16]

This erosion of political participation is not simply a reflection of apathy; it is a symptom of deeper disconnection. When people feel unrepresented, or that their vote will not translate into meaningful change, they withdraw. They don't make an active decision to disengage; rather, it's a natural response to feeling excluded. A sense of powerlessness sets in, and with it comes mistrust of politicians, institutions and even neighbours. The danger is that democratic legitimacy will begin to erode in the very communities that most need a strong, responsive state.

This disengagement can become self-perpetuating. As turnout drops, so too does political attention. Political parties focus their efforts and resources on swing constituencies and those with high-participation rates, because, let's face it, these are the people who are going to keep them in power, not the ones who don't vote because they are so disillusioned by the system. This reinforces the neglect of 'left behind' places. These communities, already grappling with declining public services, limited access to training and stalled infrastructure investment, are then further marginalised in the political imagination. Over time, that invisibility feeds resentment which creates fertile ground for anti-establishment sentiment and political volatility.

The implications of that resentment go well beyond politics. They're social. Civic withdrawal tends to go hand-in-hand with lower trust in local authorities, reduced volunteerism, weaker community ties and greater isolation. When people feel their voices aren't heard and their prospects don't matter, they're less likely to invest in their communities through collective efforts or long-term planning. That makes it ever harder for them to embrace the promise that progress is shared by the community, and everyone has a stake in the future. It really doesn't help that we are surrounded by signs of progress and technology that promises to make our lives 'easier' and 'better', even as inequality widens. Who wants to hear about AI generating amazing art while they're struggling to pay their rent, or that predictive analytics is outstanding at optimising logistics while queueing at a food bank? In the absence of a sense of shared stakes in the future, extremism finds a willing audience. Insecurity creates space for simplistic answers to complex problems: *'Someone is to blame'*; *'The system is rigged'*; *'Why bother?'* These narratives fill the vacuum left by neglect. When mainstream politics no longer speaks to most people's lived experience, alternative populist movements, often fuelled by anger and exclusion, find many willing followers. We are already seeing widespread examples of this.

Adding to the seeming hopelessness of the situation, AI appears poised to exacerbate this spiral into alternative political movements. It has already created a world saturated with information created by anyone, anywhere, all too often based on opinion and devoid of facts. The same algorithms that keep us entertained also feed each user a version of the world optimised for engagement, not truth. When AI systems can fabricate images, voices, and entire narratives indistinguishable from reality, it's impossible to know what to believe and easier to choose our own truth. Fact-checking, if it is done at all, is often reactive, appearing long after the fabricated stories they correct. By that time though, the damage is already done.

In this ecosystem, the downtrodden, over-whelmed and disoriented could retreat into smaller circles of belief, taking refuge in political tribes, influencer cults and algorithmic echo chambers. This is the real danger we are facing. Indeed, we are already seeing real signs of the early stages of the pattern I just described, with tens of thousands protesting on the streets, looking for scapegoats. Fewer and fewer people believe they are part of something worth shaping or included in their nation's story.

Facing the precipice

We already have a great deal of evidence of where the current situation will lead. In many of the 'left behind' regions from previous economic shocks, we can see a profound impact on well-being and mental health. Public health data shows that the areas with the most acute jobless figures also face the highest rates of poverty and long-term illness. Among men between the ages of 25 and 45 who left school without any qualifications or gained stable employment since, the mental health toll is especially pronounced. Rates of depression, anxiety and suicide have surged. Between 2019 and early 2023, the numbers of people economically inactive due to long-term illness increased markedly, and among those affected over half (53%) reported depression, bad nerves or anxiety. In that same period, depression and related conditions rose by roughly 40%, indicating that mental health impacts are got sharply worse since COVID.[17] Unemployment is closely linked to spikes in mood disorders, and losing a job can trigger what turns out to be a lifelong struggle with mental illness.[18] Men in traditionally male-dominated sectors – such as manufacturing, construction or transport – report disproportionately high levels of depression when they lose their jobs.[19]

If jobs are lost at the scale predicted, the number of regions that feel 'left behind' will multiply, as will the corresponding fallout-related issues. Work is about so much more than income. It gives us structure, self-worth and a sense of purpose. When those vanish, the human cost can be staggering. The challenge is not figuring out whether the change will happen – because it will – but figuring out whether we can build a coherent response quickly enough to smooth what will otherwise be a very rocky transition.

Afterword

The forces reshaping our lives, and the very fabric of society, are not abstract. AI is already here, changing everything we do in our offices, classrooms, hospitals and homes. Each new development further rewrites the rhythms of everyday life and redraws the map of opportunity. We're all impacted by it, and if you haven't yet experienced firsthand just how much the old coordinates of stability – such as career, expertise and experience – are shifting beneath your feet, you soon will be. My hope is that these changes will be positive, but there is every chance they will not.

We all need to be prepared

One of the biggest dangers of AI-led disruption is paralysis. As I've shown in this book, there is zero point in waiting for governments or corporations to step in and save us from the negative consequences of AI systems they barely control. The uncomfortable truth is that no government could manage this transition alone, even if they had the motivation to do so – and all the signs suggest they do not. They can introduce white papers, produce new (mostly toothless) regulation and maybe even give the odd tech giant a public slap on the wrist while quietly bowing to them behind closed doors.

There are many factors behind this government failure to act, but they all boil down to the same truth: we cannot rely on our elected leaders to manage or mitigate the economic shock we are hurtling towards. We cannot put our heads in the sand and say this is someone else's problem to solve. History shows that real change rarely comes from the top-down alone. The biggest shifts are spurred by individual conviction, community energy and cultural momentum.

This is where our contribution will make a massive difference.

The task of managing this transition, therefore, belongs to all of us. Every business owner, worker, educator, entrepreneur, artist and citizen has a role to play in shaping what technology becomes. Innovation can be great in all its forms, but we don't need to be passive recipients. We can help direct how innovations are used and decide how we want to shape the AI era. The first step is understanding what we are dealing with, so we can be fully prepared. AI may not destroy all jobs, but it will certainly destroy many assumptions. It will force us to confront which parts of work are essential and which parts are just habit. That doesn't have to be a bad thing.

Skilled labour is the future

Many of the clues to the future of work lead to skilled labour – people who have the skills to wire, weld, dig, design and problem-solve in real time. This reality will force many people to completely change their mindset. When it comes to career choices, skilled labour has long been seen as the poor relation to office-based, graduate-led jobs, and as a result young people are being mistakenly ushered towards university to train for jobs that are unlikely to exist when they graduate because, today, the old certainties no longer hold. Many office-based jobs are in danger of becoming obsolete, thanks to digital programs that perform required tasks quicker and cheaper than human workers. We are already seeing evidence of the fallout from this industry by industry. When AI transforms white-collar industries, it won't be a degree that protects white-collar jobs. It will be the worker's adaptability, fluency in hybrid tasks and ability to think, fix, make and move. When economic downturns hit, those with relevant tradeable skills, such as coders and technicians, will be the ones still in demand.

This is not about romanticising manual labour or pitting it against the knowledge labour. It's a call to action to recognise that technical skills and digital literacy are becoming the true currencies of resilience that will help us stay ahead in the AI era. The person who can install, repair and problem-solve across domains will always have a place in the jobs market. For young people entering an uncertain working scene, building up a skill is rapidly becoming the smartest investment they can make. While many of the jobs of the future may not even exist yet – and we might not even be able to imagine what they are – maintaining our capacity to learn, adapt, and apply knowledge in the real world is the only way to stay ahead. The greatest danger AI poses, as we've explored throughout this book, is not that machines will outthink us, but that we will underestimate ourselves in comparison to them. We must not risk mistaking AI automation for inevitable joblessness, as if progress were something happening to us rather than through us. We shouldn't let fear harden into fatalism.

Building resilience to AI

The story of technology does not need to be one of human replacement, but we humans do need to get our relationship with technology right. Every tool from the plough to the printing press has reshaped the human experience, but each depended on our ability to use it wisely. AI is no different. It can narrow our horizons or expand them. The deciding factor will not be the intelligence of the machine, but the intelligence and resilience of the society that wields it. This is why the next stage of this journey must shift focus from what AI *can* do to what we *choose* to do with it. If *The AI Alarm Bell* is a call to awareness, then *Answering the Alarm: Putting Human Value Back at the Centre of the Economy*, the next book in this trilogy, is a call to action. It explores how investment in collaboration and social infrastructure will turn technological capacity into human capability and asks how we can redirect innovation toward shared prosperity and how work itself can become a source of renewal, not just survival.

The stakes are huge and worth playing for. That's because the future of work is the future of society, encompassing vital themes such as belonging, identity and meaning. If we blindly accept AI as an all-powerful cost-saving measure, we will inherit an efficient but hollow civilisation. Alternatively, we could use it as a tool to augment human ingenuity and expand the boundaries of imagination. The question, then, is not whether AI will change the world. It already has. The question is whether we will change ourselves to meet that change. To do this, we need to keep asking 'why' and acting on the answers we find.

Notes

1. Skillicorn, N, 'Evidence that children become less creative over time (and how to fix it)', Idea to Value (5 August 2016), www.ideatovalue.com/crea/nickskillicorn/2016/08/evidence-children-become-less-creative-time-fix, accessed 21 January 2026
2. 'Research project: Sorting into tertiary education: Lessons from the UK', European University Institute (n.d.), www.eui.eu/research-hub?id=sorting-into-tertiary-education-lessons-from-the-uk, accessed 21 January 2026
3. Bolton, P, 'Research Briefing: Higher education student numbers', UK Parliament (7 January 2026), https://commonslibrary.parliament.uk/research-briefings/cbp-7857, accessed 21 January 2026
4. 'Tony Blair's full speech', *The Guardian* (28 September 1999) www.theguardian.com/politics/1999/sep/28/labourconference.labour14, accessed 21 January 2026
5. 'Research Briefing: Student loan statistics', UK Parliament (10 December 2025), https://commonslibrary.parliament.uk/research-briefings/sn01079, accessed 21 January 2026
6. Sodha, S, 'Students are racking up huge debts, but how can they tell if it's value for money?' *The Guardian* (11 February 2024), www.theguardian.com/commentisfree/2024/feb/11/why-go-to-university-when-its-almost-impossible-to-pay-off-a-student-loan, accessed 21 January 2026
7. DoNotPay: https://donotpay.com
8. Sweney, M, 'Mirror publisher puts 600 jobs at risk amid AI and reader changes', *The Guardian* (8 September 2025), www.theguardian.com/business/2025/sep/08/mirror-publisher-jobs-ai-reach-express-star, accessed 21 January 2026

9. Kinder, M, 'Hollywood writers went on strike to protect their livelihoods from generative AI. Their remarkable victory matters for all workers', Brookings (12 April 2024), www.brookings.edu/articles/hollywood-writers-went -on-strike-to-protect-their-livelihoods-from-generative -ai-their-remarkable-victory-matters-for-all-workers, accessed 21 January 2026

10. Adams, P, 'Agencies to replace 7.5% of jobs with AI by 2030 – but creatives could be spared', Marketing Dive (22 June 2023), www.marketingdive.com/news/advertising -agencies-automate-jobs-generative-AI/653499, accessed 21 January 2026

11. 'Future of Jobs Report, 2023: Insight Report', World Economic Forum (May 2023), www3.weforum.org/docs/WEF _Future_of_Jobs_2023.pdf, accessed 22 January 2026

12. 'Energy demand from AI', IEA (2025), www.iea.org/reports /energy-and-ai/energy-demand-from-ai, accessed 22 January 2026

13. Kemene, E, Valkhof, B and Greene-Dewasmes, G, 'AI and energy: Will AI help reduce emissions or increase power demand? Here's what to know', World Economic Forum (22 July 2024), www.weforum.org/stories/2024 /07/generative-ai-energy-emissions, accessed 22 January 2026

14. Calvert, B, 'AI already uses as much energy as a small country. It's only the beginning. The energy needed to support data storage is expected to double by 2026. You can do something to stop it', Vox (28 March 2024), www .vox.com/climate/2024/3/28/24111721/climate-ai-tech -energy-demand-rising, accessed 22 January 2026

15. 'The Current Status of the AI Act: Navigating the Future of AI Regulation in the EU', Stibbe (31 May 2025), www .stibbe.com/publications-and-insights/the-current-status -of-the-ai-act-navigating-the-future-of-ai-regulation, accessed 22 January 2026

16. Booth, R, '"Voting is not on their radar": lowest turnout predicted in poorest areas', The Guardian (1 May 2024), www.theguardian.com/politics/2024/may/01/voting-is -not-on-their-radar-lowest-turnout-predicted-in-poorest -areas, accessed 22 January 2026

17. Lelii, M, O'Brien, L and Hancock, L, 'Rising ill-health and economic inactivity because of long-term sickness, UK: 2019 to 2023', ONS (26 July 2023), www.ons.gov

.uk/employmentandlabourmarket/peoplenotinwork
/economicinactivity/articles/risingillhealthandecono
micinactivitybecauseoflongtermsicknessuk/2019to2023,
accessed 9 February 2026

18. Biswas, MM, Das, KC and Sheikh, I, 'Psychological
implications of unemployment among higher educated
migrant youth in Kolkata City, India', *Scientific Reports*,
14/10171 (2024), www.nature.com/articles/s41598-024
-60958-y, accessed 22 January 2026

19. Roche, AM et al. 'Men, work, and mental health: A
systematic review of depression in male-dominated
industries and occupations', *Safety and Health At Work*, 7/4
(2016), 268–283, https://pmc.ncbi.nlm.nih.gov/articles
/PMC5127922, accessed 22 January 2026

Acknowledgements

This book was not written in isolation, even if much of it was typed alone.

First and foremost, I want to thank the Elect team. Endless conversations, debates, challenges, and deep dives into AI, economics and the direction of the world have shaped this work more than any single article or dataset ever could. Mindu Bendikas and Neil Barrett were my constant sparring partners on AI and technology, questioning assumptions, stress-testing ideas, and pushing the thinking far beyond surface-level commentary. Tony Wilson, Phil Brown, Richard McMurrough and Adam Matich helped ground those ideas, bringing perspective on how these forces will truly affect people, businesses and society. The quality of thinking in this book is a direct reflection of the quality of those conversations.

To my wife, Claire; thank you for your unwavering support, for the patience, the belief and the quiet understanding that writing a book isn't just about time at a desk, but time away from everything else. Your support has been constant, even when the process wasn't.

To Niamh and Max, thank you for letting me see the world through your eyes. I cherish your inquisitive minds, your willingness to challenge ideas and your refusal to accept that I'm right simply because I'm your dad. You remind me daily that the future doesn't belong to those who think they have all the answers, but to those brave enough to keep asking better questions.

And finally, to Teena Lyons, thank you for being present throughout this entire journey and for helping shape a narrative around my views, for the conversations, the structure, and the ability to turn raw thought into something coherent, readable and human. This book is better because you were part of the process from start to finish.

The Author

Phil Taylor-Guck is an entrepreneur, investor and author with a background in finance and economics. He is the founder and CEO of the Elect Group, a multidisciplinary business spanning recruitment, training, social value and investment, with a focus on workforce transformation and long-term value creation. Phil's work explores the intersection of economics, labour markets, AI and social systems, challenging prevailing narratives around work, wealth and opportunity. Known for asking uncomfortable questions and resisting simplistic answers, his writing blends data, systems thinking and real-world experience. He is a husband and father of two, drawing inspiration from curiosity, challenge and critical thought.

You can connect with Phil Taylor-Guck via:

🌐 electholdings.com